GLOBAL PROFILES

LATIN AMERICAN WRITERS

Lynn Shirey

☑® Facts On File, Inc.

For Ricardo and Danielito

Latin American Writers

Facts On File, Inc.
11 Penn Plaza
New York NY 10001

Library of Congress Cataloging-in-Publication Data

Shirey, Lynn.
   Latin American writers / Lynn Shirey.
     p. cm. — (Global profiles)
   Includes bibliographical references and index.
   Contents: Jorge Luis Borges (1899–1986) — Gabriel García Márquez (1927 or 1928–) — Jorge Amado (1912–) — Carlos Fuentes (1928–) — Julio Cortázar (1914–1984) — Rosario Castellanos (1925–1974) — Mario Vargas Llosa (1936–) — Isabel Allende (1942–).
   Summary: A collective biography profiling the lives of eight Latin American writers, including Jorge Luis Borges, Gabriel García Márquez, Jorge Amado, and Isabel Allende.
   ISBN 0-8160-3202-5
   1. Authors, Latin American—20th century—Biography—Juvenile literature.
2. Latin American literature—20th century—History and criticism—Juvenile literature.   [1. Authors, Latin American.]
I. Title.   II. Series.
PQ7081.3.S45 1997
860.9—dc20   96-18378

Text design by Catherine Rincon Hyman
Cover design by Nora Wertz

This book is printed on acid-free paper.

Printed in the United States of America

MP FOF 10 9 8 7 6 5 4 3 2 1

Contents

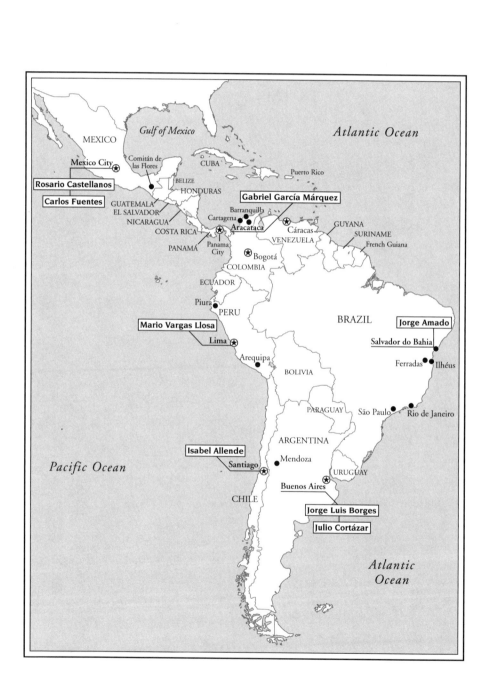

MEXICO

Gulf of Mexico

Atlantic Ocean

Mexico City ⊛

Comitán de
las Flores

CUBA

Puerto Rico

Rosario Castellanos

BELIZE

Carlos Fuentes

GUATEMALA
EL SALVADOR
NICARAGUA

HONDURAS

Gabriel García Márquez

Barranquilla

COSTA RICA

Cartagena

PANAMÁ

Panama
City

⊛

Aracataca

Cáracas

GUYANA

SURINAME

French Guiana

VENEZUELA

⊛ Bogotá

COLOMBIA

ECUADOR

Piura

PERU

BRAZIL

Jorge Amado

Mario Vargas Llosa

Lima ⊛

Salvador do Bahia

Arequipa

BOLIVIA

Ferradas

Ilhéus

PARAGUAY

São Paulo

Rio de Janeiro

ARGENTINA

Isabel Allende

Santiago

⊛

Mendoza

URUGUAY

CHILE

Buenos Aires

⊛

Jorge Luis Borges

Julio Cortázar

Pacific Ocean

Atlantic
Ocean

Introduction

In the 1960s a handful of Latin American writers captured the world's attention with imaginative and powerful new works of fiction. Their novels and stories were translated from the Spanish and Portuguese into many languages and became international best-sellers. This explosion of creativity is now known as the "boom" in Latin American literature.

Until the 1960s, there was no such term as "Latin American literature," although there were long traditions of Argentine, Mexican, Brazilian and other literatures from individual countries. Each of the 21 Spanish- and Portuguese-speaking nations of Latin America had its own writers, subjects and literary styles.

Most of the countries of Latin America were governed by Spain and Portugal from the early 1500s. They remained European colonies for more than 300 years, until they fought for and won their independence in the 19th century. Years of revolution were followed by civil wars and occasional frontier battles with the native peoples.

By the beginning of the 20th century, these were proud and modern nations with diverse cultures and heritages. Their citizens were immigrants from all parts of Europe, who to varying degrees had mixed with the indigenous populations. Today, Spanish is still the official language nearly everywhere in Latin America, except in Brazil, which once belonged to Portugal, and in some former English, French and Dutch colonies.

Each of these countries is unique. They vary greatly in climate and geography, and the native inhabitants of each region have distinct languages and customs. In some places, slaves were imported from Africa until the mid-19th century. All of these elements helped to form the new nations' identities.

After independence was won in the mid-1800s, local customs and traditions were celebrated proudly. Literature, like music and the arts, reflected each country's individuality, tastes and interests. While poetry, essays, stories and novels had local themes and subjects, they were still very European in style and tradition.

The modern Latin American writers described in this book rebelled against old-fashioned European conventions. They created imaginative new works that attracted the attention of readers and critics throughout the world. Although each of these authors is unique, they share certain experiences and convictions about life and art.

Most of them developed new styles and techniques: Some stories are told by many or all of the characters instead of by one all-knowing narrator; events unfold out of order or begin again at the story's end; flashbacks and other devices from film are used; some novels take the form of puzzles, scrapbooks and collages.

These stories and novels were no longer set exclusively in Latin America: Many authors spent long periods in exile because of domestic political violence, and their characters often appear in stories set in Paris, London, Rome or Barcelona where the authors lived. Even Jorge Luis Borges, who lived in Argentina for most of his life, often wrote about foreign or even imaginary places.

Each writer profiled in this book broke the established rules of literature in some way or another. Humor, a powerful instrument of change, is an important element in Latin American fiction. Julio Cortázar, Gabriel García Márquez,

Jorge Amado and Mario Vargas Llosa each has his own brand of slapstick and irony. Some of these writers play with genres, or types of fiction—Borges combines detective stories with fantasy, and Vargas Llosa mixes real life with radio soap operas and historical events.

Magical realism is the best known of the new styles associated with Latin American fiction. It combines realistic, everyday detail with mysterious events, fantastic images and dreams. The result is not fantasy but a new kind of realism.

Gabriel García Márquez is the writer who is best known for magical realism. Readers all over the world know his old man with wings, the girl blown away with the wash on a windy day, and his rainstorms of frogs and dead birds. Jorge Amado and Isabel Allende have created their own magical images and worlds as well. Magic and imagination are important elements in the works of all these writers.

As children, all of these writers loved books. Their favorites were tales of adventure and travel in faraway places. Jorge Luis Borges and Carlos Fuentes came from educated families who encouraged them to read. Others, like Isabel Allende, Jorge Amado and García Márquez, discovered books on their own. Rosario Castellanos had to steal volumes from her father's library and read them in secret.

In Latin America, it is common for novelists and poets to write for newspapers and magazines. Mario Vargas Llosa, Isabel Allende, Jorge Amado and Gabriel García Márquez occasionally worked as journalists in order to make a living, and all of these writers have expressed their ideas about art and politics to the press throughout their careers.

Latin America has been plagued by repression, military coups, kidnappings, torture and injustice throughout the 20th century. Each of these writer's lives has been touched by this violence in some way. Isabel Allende was forced into exile after the brutal 1973 military coup in Chile. Jorge Amado was imprisoned and exiled from his country on several occasions. Cortázar and Borges lost jobs because they opposed the politics of former Argentine president Juan Domingo Perón. All made enemies of their governments at one time or other, and their books were sometimes burned or prohibited.

Many of these writers were active in politics; some still are today. Cortázar, Fuentes, García Márquez, Amado and Vargas Llosa were all strong supporters of the Cuban Revolution of 1959; although some have changed their political views, they continue to discuss them passionately. Fuentes and Castellanos were both Mexican ambassadors, and Amado was a deputy for the Brazilian Communist Party. Vargas Llosa recently ran for (and lost) the presidency of Peru. García Márquez continues to work for international human rights organizations.

These writers share a deep sense of responsibility toward their countries. They have the power of words and the ability to speak to many. In their fiction, in the press and in their lives, they have always spoken out against social injustice.

These contemporary Latin American writers revolutionized their national literatures with their deep social concerns, new techniques and imaginative styles. Modern writers from all over the world have been influenced by them as well. Magical realism has begun to appear in fiction from the United States, Great Britain and many other places.

These writers are not only talented; they are also popular. Their novels and stories are entertaining and often fun. People everywhere identify with their characters and situations. Some works are more difficult to read than others and require more patience. Many can be read in more than one way—as love stories, political satires or tales of adventure.

The writers whose lives are described in this book represent only a few of the many fine contemporary writers from Latin America. They are among the best known, for their works have been translated internationally. Many good novels and stories remain untranslated and are a marvelous incentive for the non-Spanish or non-Portuguese speaker to learn these languages.

Jorge Luis Borges at Harvard University, where he was professor of poetry from 1967 to 1968   (Courtesy of the Harvard News Office)

Jorge Luis Borges

THE PUZZLE OF THE UNIVERSE
(1899–1986)

The most important Latin American writer of the 20th century is Jorge Luis Borges. His imaginative stories inspired writers everywhere. Now classics of Latin American fiction, they are known internationally for their power and originality.

Borges's stories were among the first to blend fantasy with reality and dream with logic. They begin with precise descriptions of historical events, facts and real people and things, but these soon give way to mystery and uncertainty. His characters are often doubles of each other, though they seem like opposites. Events repeat themselves, and time stands still. Stories are enclosed within stories and dreams within dreams. As in detective fiction, there are plot twists and surprise endings.

Borges was born in Buenos Aires, Argentina, in 1899. His ancestors included military heroes of the Indian wars and Argentina's battles for independence from Spain. His father, Jorge Guillermo Borges, was well educated and earned a living as a lawyer, translator, teacher and writer. His mother, Leonor Acevedo, translated several major works of North American fiction into Spanish. Important writers and poets of the time were daily visitors to the household. The Borges were a family who fed on language.

Young Borges was frail and timid and wore glasses from an early age. His only real friend was his younger sister Norah. Obsessed with adventure and travel in distant lands, he rarely left the family home. He explored the entire world from within the walls of his father's magnificent library.

Borges's father was half English, and very proud of it. Both English and Spanish were spoken in the Borges home, and Jorge (or "Georgie" as he was called) knew both languages well. Until the age of nine, he was taught at home by an English tutor. The great library was full of English-language books; among Borges's early favorites were the tales of Robert Louis Stevenson, Rudyard Kipling, Edgar Allan Poe and Mark Twain, which he read in English.

Borges often felt like an alien while he was growing up. The family lived in Palermo, an old neighborhood of Buenos Aires that was then on the outermost edge of the city. A violent place, it was home to knife fighters and criminals. His middle-class family was out of place there, and the shy, bookish boy who spoke English was even more so.

Parents of great writers everywhere often object to their children's choice of career; writers seldom earn much money at first and sometimes lead precarious, unsettled lives. But Borges was lucky—his family always expected him to become a writer and encouraged him in many ways. His father, a frustrated writer himself, was kept from his ambitions by his worsening blindness. Borges would also grow blind in his later years, victim of the same hereditary disease, but by the age of six he had begun to write his own imaginative tales. At nine, his translation from English of

"If I were asked to name the chief event in my life, I should say my father's library."

Oscar Wilde's story "The Happy Prince" was printed in *El País*, a local newspaper. Signed *Jorge Borges*, everyone assumed it to be his father's work. At 13, he published his first short story, "King of the Jungle." It is an unusual tale, told from the point of view of a proud tiger stalked by a mysterious hunter.

Borges's grandmother on his father's side was English. Frances ("Fanny") Haslam had lived with the family as long as he could remember and was an important influence on the young boy. She had traveled to Argentina from England in the late 1800s to visit her elder sister, who was living there. In 1870, she met Colonel Francisco Borges, a heroic commander of the government forces during one of Argentina's civil wars. They were married soon after and had two sons, the younger being Borges's father. When the colonel was killed by an enemy bullet in 1874, Fanny Haslam chose to remain in Argentina. Her wonderful stories of battles, gauchos (cowboys of the *pampa*, or plains) and the frontier days sparked young Borges's imagination. She had an ironic sense of humor that Borges admired, and he often claimed that her style of storytelling was the origin of his own.

In 1914, the Borges family traveled to Europe, where Borges's father was to have eye surgery. They planned to live in Paris for a while, but World War I broke out when they were in Geneva, Switzerland. Travel became unsafe, and they remained there for four years. Borges enrolled in the College de Genève, a private secondary school where classes were given in French and Latin. He learned these languages quickly and also taught himself German as well. He admired the German Expressionist poets and was the first to translate their works into Spanish.

Borges took his high school diploma 1918. It was the last formal education he ever received. Few people realize that one of the most intellectual and learned writers of the 20th century was almost entirely self-taught.

The Borges family moved to Spain that same year. On the island of Majorca, Borges helped his father write a novel about the Argentine civil war of the 1870s. It was at this time that he also began to write seriously. His first efforts were poems, which he wrote in English and French, but he finally decided that Spanish was the language in which he expressed himself best.

His poems soon began to appear in Spanish magazines. By 1920, he had become part of a literary circle that met regularly at Madrid's Café Colonial to discuss and read new literature. Led by Spanish poet Rafael Cansinos-Asséns and promoting a new style of writing called *ultraísmo*, the group's goal was to replace the old fashioned, romantic styles of the past with modern forms. At first, the long nights of passionate conversation were exciting for Borges, but he soon decided that he preferred not to belong to any one tradition or group.

Borges's father gave him good advice about writing: "Read a lot, write a lot, tear up a lot, and don't be in any hurry to publish." In Spain, Borges wrote a volume each of poems and essays, which he soon came to view as idealistic and romantic; on the eve of his departure for Argentina, he destroyed them.

When the Borges family returned to Buenos Aires in March 1921, they found a very different place than that they had left seven years before—a growing, modern city instead of a comfortable, intimate town. Borges was amazed at this change and felt deep nostalgia for the city's past. This experience led to his first book of poetry, *Fervor de Buenos Aires* (*Fervor of Buenos Aires*), published in 1923.

At the time, most books were printed privately, instead of by publishing houses. Borges's father paid to have 300 copies of *Fervor* printed, and his sister Norah made an engraving for the cover (she later became a well-known artist). Because Borges was unknown, no bookstores would sell his book. But one day while visiting the offices of *Nosotros* (Us), an established literary magazine, he noticed some coats of important visitors hanging in the waiting room. He quietly slipped copies of his book into their pockets. Borges then went away to Switzerland with his family, where his father was to have further eye surgery. When they returned to Buenos Aires a year later, Borges found that he was known as a poet!

The 1920s were years of great activity for Borges. In 1921, he founded *Prisma*, a publication designed as a "mural-magazine": Borges and his friends printed several poems and a literary "manifesto," or declaration about literary ideas, on one large sheet of paper; then they slipped out at night and pasted it on the walls and fences of Buenos Aires as a gift to its citizens. They couldn't, however, afford to publish this free magazine for long, and in 1922, Borges joined forces with a group of new writers and founded another literary magazine called *Proa*. More important than the magazine itself were the lifelong friendships that he forged while working on it. In 1924, he began to write for *Martín Fierro*, a satirical, modernist literary review, and in the 1930s, he collaborated on the magazine *Sur* (South), founded by his friend Victoria O'Campo.

In 1925 and 1929, Borges published more poetry in volumes entitled *Luna de enfrente* (Moon across the way) and *Cuadernos de San Martín* (San Martín notebook) and wrote essays on such topics as old Buenos Aires, literature, language and film. Throughout his long career, Borges published at least 20 volumes of essays and poetry and edited several anthologies of fantastic and detective literature.

"When I came back after a year's absence, I found that some of the overcoats had read my poems, and a few had even written about them. As a matter of fact, in this way I got myself a small reputation as a poet."

It is Borges's fiction, however, that is known throughout the world. In 1933, he published his first prose collection, *Historia universal de la infamia* (*The Universal History of Infamy*), short, imaginative versions of famous thieves' and outlaws' real lives. The well-known Billy the Kid, a gangster named Monk Eastman and Tom Castro, a famous impersonator, were a few of the collection's subjects. In both style and technique, these pieces foreshadowed his later fiction.

All of Borges's stories are brief, usually only a few pages long. He never wrote a novel; in fact, he believed that most novels were too long and only repeated one or two basic ideas. In his own writing, he strove for an exact, precise form of expression. This precision is one of the sources of their power.

The late 1930s and the 1940s were the most difficult years in Borges's long life: Illness, death, and economic and political problems shattered his formerly peaceful existence; his grandmother Fanny Haslam died in 1935 at the age of 90; a depression that struck the previously prosperous Argentina in the 1930s affected the Borges household as well.

Borges had several unhappy love affairs in the 1920s but never married. In the 1930s, he was still living at his parents' home, and it became necessary for him to help with the family finances. His occasional writing and editing jobs earned him only small sums of money.

In 1937, he was hired as a librarian by a small public library. He worked there for the next nine years, later describing them as "solid unhappiness." His coworkers complained that he worked too hard and made them look bad. In response, he completed his tasks hurriedly and then escaped for hours each day to a basement office to read and write in secret. While he never became immensely popular, his fame as a writer began to grow. However, no one at the library ever suspected he was the same Borges who wrote stories!

Two tragedies occurred in 1938. First, Borges's beloved father died. Borges was deeply sorrowed by the death of this

Borges with María Kodama in Buenos Aires   (Willis Barnstone)

man, who was friend and teacher as well as parent. Then at Christmastime that same year, while climbing a dark staircase at his home, Borges struck his head against a window beam. The wound became infected and he hovered between life and death for a month in a hospital.

As Borges began to recover, his eyesight quickly worsened, and he worried that he had lost his ability to write. Instead of returning to poetry and essays, he decided to try something new. The stories he wrote during the next 10 years were a mixture of nightmare and reality that may well have emerged from his illness and were the best of his entire career.

Ficciones (1944) and *El Aleph* (*The Aleph*, 1949) contain many of his best stories. None of Borges's stories is easily categorized. Most are mixes of fantasy, mystery, adventure and philosophy. They have powerful, often nightmarish moods, and the strange events that occur always have more than one explanation.

In many of these stories, the narrator (usually Borges himself) begins by chatting in an everyday voice. Sometimes, Borges has received some news in a letter or has discovered the story's key element on a page from a lost manuscript. In "Tlön, Uqbar, Orbis Tertius," Borges tells us how he and a friend discover a strange entry for a place called Uqbar in an encyclopedia volume. Together, they uncover a plot by a secret society to create a perfect but fantastic world.

Dream and reality are the themes of "Las ruinas circulares" ("The Circular Ruins"). The tone is mysterious and mythlike:

> No one saw him disembark in the unanimous night, no one saw the bamboo canoe sinking into the sacred mud, but within a few days no one was unaware that the silent man came from the South and that his home was one of the infinite villages upstream, on the violent mountainside, where the Zend tongue is not contaminated with Greek and where leprosy is infrequent.

The man discovers the ruins of an ancient temple where he sets about creating a man by dreaming him. He eventually succeeds but discovers that he, too, has been dreamed by another. Many of Borges's stories can be read several ways. This one is a horror story but a mystery as well. Once the ending is known, a rereading of the puzzling text shows many clues that point to the final surprise.

"The Circular Ruins" contains some of the philosophical ideas that underlie most of Borges's fiction. Borges was interested in the idea of the universe as a puzzle. Reality is not what it seems but is a series of clues to what lies beyond. People and events are never unique but are doubles and ghosts of others. Above all, time is an illusion. Borges learned these ideas from the works of Greek philosopher Plato and from such Eastern religions as Taoism and Zen.

Most of Borges's characters are men of action—spies, gauchos, soldiers, bandits or gunmen. This choice is curious because Borges was such a timid, bookish person—but he was interested in history, especially in the dramatic moment when a character choses his destiny.

"La forma de la espada" ("The Shape of the Sword") tells of a hero and a traitor in Ireland's rebellion against England in 1916. "El jardín de senderos que se bifurcan" ("The Garden of Forking Paths") is on one level a spy story about a Chinese man who works for the Germans in England during the war, but it also interweaves the discovery of a lost labyrinth (a book), the character of an English scholar and a murder.

The labyrinth, or maze, is an important image in many of Borges's stories; he was fascinated with the one inhabited by the Minotaur in Greek mythology. Labyrinths are puzzles composed of connecting paths: one leads to a hidden center, while all the others lead to dead ends. Borges's stories are like labyrinths: They present mysteries whose solutions can be arrived at in several ways.

Borges saw reality as a great mystery that could never be explained. His stories often have unclear endings that hint at other meanings, other paths. The plots are full of gaps, and the characters are often ambiguous. They are often Borges's memory of a story someone told him or of a popular legend of which no one knows the origin. He offers partial explanations but leaves the reader to find his own meaning.

In the midst of his greatest creative activity, Borges began to have political problems. Although never an outspoken critic of Argentina's government, he didn't hide his dislike of the dictator Juan Domingo Perón, who came into power in 1946. Perón was strongly nationalistic and attacked all cultural institutions and individuals whose work showed European influence, including most Argentine intellectuals and writers of the time. Perón relieved Borges of his library job and cruelly appointed him "Inspector of Poultry and Rabbits in the Public Markets." Of course, Borges resigned immediately.

Luckily, Borges had loyal friends who arranged a teaching position for him at the Instituto Anglo-Argentino, a British school. He lectured on English and American literature there and throughout Argentina and Uruguay. At first, he was very nervous about speaking in public and practiced his speeches before his mother. But he soon found that he enjoyed lecturing and became a popular speaker. In his free time, Borges continued writing stories, poetry and essays.

Borges's blindness had gradually worsened. Since 1928, he had been operated on several times, though unsuccessfully. By the 1950s he had to rely on his mother and friends to read to him and to put his poems and essays down on paper.

When Perón fell from power in 1955, Borges was no longer considered dangerous. Much to his amazement, he was appointed Director of the National Library. Ironically, now that he had more books than ever within his reach, he couldn't read. He worked there for almost 20 years, resigning in 1973 in protest of Perón's return to power.

In 1956, he also became professor of English and American literature at the University of Buenos Aires. At this time, he was writing less fiction than before, probably because dictating it to someone else was so difficult, but he continued to write poems, essays and what he called *Parables*, short meditations on literary themes.

Although Borges was well-respected among his literary friends, he was never very popular in Argentina. His stories were different from anything that had been published before. Argentines were used to realistic tales that glorified their customs. Borges's concern with philosophy, along with his international characters and settings, were often criticized.

Fame came to Borges late in life and from abroad. When his stories were translated into English and French in the 1960s, he quickly became a celebrity. He was invited to lecture, teach and give interviews internationally. In 1961, he was awarded the prestigious Prix Formentor, a European publishers' prize that he shared with the Irish playwright Samuel Beckett. The universities of Oxford (England), Michigan and Columbia each granted Borges honorary doctorates. French president General Charles de Gaulle bestowed on him the title of Commander of the Order of Letters and Arts, and Queen Elizabeth appointed him a knight of the British Empire. In 1976 Borges addressed the United States Congress on the subject of Shakespeare.

Because of his blindness, it seemed as if Borges would never write fiction again, but in 1960 he published *El Hacedor* (*Dreamtigers*), a collection of stories and poems, and in 1970, another anthology, *El informe de Brodie* (*Doctor Brodie's Report*), appeared, containing what Borges called his "straightforward" stories—their plots may be simpler, but they are filled with horror, mystery and dreams. In the story "El Evangelio según Marcos" ("The Gospel According to Mark"), a young man from the city is crucified by the simple country people to whom he reads from the Bible. "La intrusa" ("The Intruder") is a chilling tale of two brothers whose friendship is threatened by a woman they both love.

Borges composed these stories in his head. He memorized each one, word for word, and then dictated them to his mother. He often said she was his best critic. Once, she wrote down a story's end before he arrived at it, and he claimed it was exactly as he had planned. She traveled with him well into her old age and was 99 when she died in 1975. Her death was a relief for everyone, for she had suffered greatly during her last two years. Just the same, for Borges the loss of his lifelong companion came as a shock.

In 1967, at the age of 68, Borges married for the first time. He had been interested in Elsa Astete de Millán in the 1920s, but she had rejected him and married someone else. When they met again, she was a widow. Their marriage was not a happy one, however, and they were divorced three years later.

During the 1960s, Borges met María Kodama, a student in his class at the University of Buenos Aires. At first she was intimidated by his renown and wanted to drop out of his course, but he convinced her to stay and they soon became friends. For the next 20 years Kodama worked as Borges's assistant. This position involved reading to him, writing down his poems, stories and essays, and traveling with him when his mother no longer could. In time their relationship deepened; some of his last writings were the love poems he dedicated to her.

"I do not write for a select minority, which means nothing to me, nor for that adulated platonic entity known as 'The Masses' . . . I write for myself and for my friends, and I write to ease the passing of time."

Despite his blindness, Borges was a healthy man with a lively and curious mind. Toward the end of his life, he traveled widely with Kodama to the exotic places he'd read about in his youth. They collaborated on a book called *Atlas*, a collection of his travel pieces and her photographs; one photo shows Borges seated on a stairway that leads into the Cretan labyrinth of Knossos, home of the fabled Minotaur. Borges and Kodama were married in Geneva, Switzerland, shortly before his death on June 14, 1986.

Jorge Luis Borges is one of the century's most influential writers. In this modern age, Borges's themes of time and memory are truly universal; his writing is a search for meaning and order in an increasingly chaotic world.

Many of the greatest Latin American writers have experimented with dream and magic and have invented new styles and techniques, but Borges's originality and precision of language inspired and stimulated them all. The Mexican novelist Carlos Fuentes summed up Borges's importance:

> The ultimate significance of Borges's prose—without which, quite simply, the modern Latin American novel would not exist—is that it attests basically to the fact that Latin America is in want of language, and that therefore it must be constituted. To do so, Borges blurs all genres, rescues all traditions, kills all bad habits, creates a new order, rigorous and demanding, on which irony, humor, and play can be built . . . and . . . constitutes a new Latin American language. . . .

Nevertheless, Borges was a controversial figure. Many of the younger writers who were or are politically active criticized Borges's silence in the face of social injustice, but he never cared for politics or reality and avoided them in his life and in his writing. It is interesting that Márquez and

Cortázar, two of Latin America's most political writers, are also those most greatly inspired by Borges's example.

For years it was rumored that Borges would receive the Nobel Prize in literature. Although he never did, many readers the world over believe that he deserved the honor.

Chronology

August 24, 1899	Jorge Luis Borges born in Buenos Aires, Argentina
1914–19	Travels to Europe with his family.
1919–21	Lives in Spain; publishes his first poems
1921	Returns to Buenos Aires
1923	Publishes his first collection of poetry, *Fervor of Buenos Aires.*
1937	Becomes assistant librarian
1946	"Promoted" from librarian to poultry inspector; resigns
1955	Becomes director of the National Library
1956	Named professor of English literature at the University of Buenos Aires
1961	Stories translated into French; awarded the Prix Formentor
1962	First works translated into English
1967	Marries Elsa Astete de Millán
1970	Divorced
1973	Resigns from National Library to protest Perón's return
1978–1984	Travels widely; *Atlas*, book of travel pieces with photographs by companion María Kodama

| May 1986 | Marries María Kodama |
| June 14, 1986 | Borges dies in Geneva, Switzerland |

Further Reading

BORGES'S WORKS

The Aleph and Other Stories, 1933–1969, Together with Commentaries and an Autobiographical Essay. Edited and translated by Norman Thomas di Giovanni in collaboration with the author. New York: Dutton, 1970. A selection of Borges's early and later stories.

Doctor Brodie's Report. Translated by Norman Thomas di Giovanni in collaboration with the author. New York: Dutton, 1972. Later stories, including "The Intruder."

Labyrinths: Selected Stories & Other Writings. Edited by Donald A. Yates & James E. Irby. New York: New Directions, 1964. Many of Borges's best known stories, along with essays and other short pieces. Good introduction, chronology and bibliography.

BOOKS ABOUT JORGE LUIS BORGES

Gene H. Bell-Villada. *Borges and His Fiction: A Guide to His Mind and Art*. Chapel Hill: The University of North Carolina Press, 1981. Very readable study of Borges's life and work.

Emir Rodríguez Monegal. *Jorge Luis Borges: A Literary Biography*. New York: Dutton, 1978. The most important biography of Borges, by a friend and colleague.

Martin S. Stabb. *Borges Revisited*. Boston: Twayne, 1991. Good study of Borges's life and major works.

Gabriel García Márquez (Palomares)

Gabriel García Márquez

CHRONICLER OF SOLITUDE
(1927 or 1928–)

A woman too beautiful for this earth vanishes with the breeze while hanging sheets out to dry. A young man's blood streams through a town until it reaches his mother's feet as she works in the kitchen. An old man with enormous wings suddenly appears amid the chickens in a barnyard. These are a few of the magical images from the stories and novels of Gabriel García Márquez, the writer who popularized magical realism.

Gabriel García Márquez was awarded the Nobel Prize in literature in 1982 for writing in which "the fantastic and the realistic are combined in a richly composed world of imagination reflecting a continent's life and conflicts." All of Latin America celebrated along with him.

At the age of 54, García Márquez was one of the youngest writers ever to win this prestigious international award. Since then, the Colombian writer has been beseiged by interview-seeking journalists and well-meaning admirers from all parts of the world. Although a good humored, generous man, he guards his solitude jealously. It is an essential ingredient in his life as a writer.

García Márquez claims that was born in 1928, although his father, in a published interview, insisted that it was 1927. In any case, his birthplace was a small town in northern Colombia called Aracataca, about 30 miles from the Caribbean Sea. This lush, tropical part of Colombia was a colorful place to grow up in: Descendants of English and Dutch pirates, African slaves and shipwrecked adventurers worked on vast banana plantations. The varied legends and customs of these diverse people mingled with the local Colombian culture, creating a wealth of material for the future writer.

Young García Márquez spent the first eight years of his life in the home of his maternal grandparents in Aracataca. Although the exact reason for this was never clear, it was true that his father and grandparents shared a troubled relationship. His father, Gabriel Eligio García, was a stranger to Aracataca when he began his determined courtship of Luisa Márquez. He had come to town in the 1920s during a banana industry boom that attracted scores of fortune-seeking immigrants. The established local people, like García Márquez's grandparents, resented the newcomers. Moreover, his grandfather had fought on the Liberal side during Colombia's civil wars. Gabriel Eligio García belonged to the opposing Conservative Party.

"I believe that the Caribbean taught me to see reality in a different way, to accept supernatural elements as forming part of our everyday life. The Caribbean is a world apart, whose first magical literary work is the diary of Christopher Columbus, a book that talks about fabulous plants and mythological worlds. . . . Not only is it the world that taught me to write, but it is also the only region where I don't feel like a foreigner."

The future author's grandparents finally consented to the marriage of Luisa and Gabriel Eligio, but only on the condition that they live away from Aracataca. They settled in Riohacha, a city on the coast, but returned to Aracataca for the birth of Gabriel on March 6, 1927 (or 1928). He was the first of their 16 children. Eventually they returned to Riohacha, leaving their firstborn in the care of his grandparents.

The boy was very close to his grandfather, Colonel Nicolás Márquez, a vital and impressive man who had fought in the War of a Thousand Days (1899–1902). This was the bloodiest of several conflicts between the followers of Colombia's Liberal and Conservative parties, and thousands of Colombians were killed. During their many long walks together, his grandfather told endless tales of heroic battles and gunfights. He treated the young boy with great respect and answered his every question. When his grandfather didn't know an answer, they would look it up together in the dictionary. They went to the circus every time it came to town. One day, his grandfather took him to see ice for the first time; García Márquez later remembered the occasion in his greatest novel, *Cien años de soledad* (*One Hundred Years of Solitude*).

García Márquez has often described his grandfather as his best friend: "Throughout my adult life, whenever something happens to me, above all whenever something good comes my way, I feel that the only thing I need in order for my happiness to be complete, is that my grandfather should know about it." The only character who resembles Colonel Márquez in his grandson's fiction is the nameless colonel of his first novel *La Hojarasca* (*Leafstorm*), but the Colonel's vivid memories of the violence of 19th-century Colombia appear in many of his grandson's works.

García Márquez's grandmother was very different from his grandfather but was also a powerful influence on the young writer's imagination. She lived in a world of myth, superstition and magic and had a great gift for storytelling.

She convinced the boy that long-dead relatives inhabited dark corners of the house. During the day, he was fascinated by her tales of ghosts and magic, but at night, he was often terrified. She told incredible stories in such a serious manner that he always believed them: "It's possible to get away with *anything*, as long as you make it believable. That is something my grandmother taught me." The author traces his fascination for magical realism, the literary style for which he later became famous, to his grandmother.

Colonel Márquez died when his grandson was almost eight years old. It was the end of the boy's childhood and the end of Aracataca as well, for in 1936 he was sent to live with his parents and younger siblings in Sucre, an inland city. García Márquez's father lacked steady work, and the growing family was often poor. Although his father had trained to be a doctor, he never finished his studies. After working early on as a telegraph operator, he eventually found a job as a pharmacologist.

García Márquez grew very close to his mother, and their relationship was very serious and important to him. She appeared briefly in her son's novel *Crónica de una muerte anunciada* (*Chronicle of a Death Foretold*). Of his father, García Márquez has never said very much, except that he never knew him well. He did, however, have a passion for reading that García Márquez seems to have inherited.

After living at home for only a few years, the young man was sent away to study. From 1940 to 1942 he at-

> "My grandmother told me the most atrocious stories without getting upset, as if they were things she had just seen. I found that her unflappable manner and rich images were what made her stories seem so real. Using the same method as my grandmother, I wrote *One Hundred Years of Solitude*."

tended a Jesuit school in Barranquilla, a coastal city. In 1943 he was awarded a scholarship to study and board at the national high school in Zipaquirá, an inland city near Bogotá.

Bogotá, Colombia's capital, was a large and bustling place even in the 1940s. On this high plateau near the Andes Mountains, the nights were cold, the people busy and reserved and the skies often gray. It was quite a different world from that of García Márquez's colorful Caribbean childhood. He disliked it intensely and escaped by reading adventure novels: The tales of Jules Verne and Emilio Salgari were some of his favorites, along with classics such as *The Three Musketeers, The Count of Monte Cristo* and *The Hunchback of Notre Dame.* Although serious and shy during his school years, he enjoyed discussing books with his classmates.

During these years, García Márquez became very interested in literature and read everything he could. His high school teachers were interested in socialist ideas for change in Latin America: "When I left there, I wanted to be a journalist, I wanted to write novels, and I wanted to do something for a more just society. The three things, I now think, were inseparable." He graduated from high school in 1946.

After summering with his family in Sucre, García Márquez enrolled in the National University in Bogotá in 1947. His father, who had never completed his own education, was anxious for his son to earn a degree. García Márquez began to study law half-heartedly, neglecting his studies and spending most of his time reading and discussing literature. That same year, his first short story, "La tercera resignación" ("The Third Resignation"), which he wrote hurriedly in response to a newspaper contest, was the published winner in the weekend edition of *El Espectador*, an important daily newspaper. It was a strange story about the death of a young boy, who continued to grow and think while inside his coffin. It was the first of 15 short stories of his that were published in several newspapers during the next five years.

The history of Colombia is a turbulent one, marked by civil war, struggles for independence and long periods of violence. In 1948 a Liberal presidential candidate was assassinated, and the country was plunged into another long period of unrest, violence and dictatorship. The university was closed, and García Márquez returned to the relative safety of the Caribbean region.

From 1948 to 1949 he continued his law studies in Cartagena de Indias; more important, he also worked as a journalist for *El Universal*, a new daily newspaper. In addition to selecting and editing news stories, he wrote numerous short articles on culture and politics, many of these unusual and humorous pieces as the history of the accordion. They tended to mix fiction with reality, just as his later fiction did. Thus began García Márquez's long career in journalism, which would take him to several foreign capitals on three continents.

In 1950, García Márquez finally gave up his law studies and moved to Barranquilla, where he worked for the newspaper *El Heraldo*. The following years, from 1950 to 1953, were immensely important in his development as a writer. He made lifelong friends among some local writers known as the "Barranquilla Group." During their long nights of lively conversation, he obtained his literary education. They discussed the great classics as well as new developments in world literature, their favorite modern authors included William Faulkner, Ernest Hemingway and Virginia Woolf.

Another very important event occurred in 1950. García Márquez returned briefly to Aracataca for the first time in many years, accompanying his mother, who was arranging to sell his grandparents' home. His grandmother had died a few years earlier while he was away at school. His reencounter with the once lively setting of his magical childhood, now decayed and empty in the tropical heat, disturbed him deeply. A powerful nostalgia for the lost world of the past overcame García Márquez, and he resolved to re-create it in his fiction.

In the following year, he wrote his first novel, *Leafstorm*, the first of his several works about Macondo, a fictitious town much like the Aracataca of his youth. The novel was initially rejected but was finally published in 1955.

García Márquez returned to Bogotá in 1954 to write for *El Espectador*, then one of the two most important daily newspapers in Colombia. He was responsible for a regular column of film reviews and began to work as an investigative reporter as well. He continued to publish short stories. In 1955 his novel *Leafstorm* finally was published, and he won the Colombian Association of Writers and Artists award for the story "One Day after Saturday." It describes the strange appearance of hundreds of dead birds in the town of Macondo.

In 1955 *El Espectador* offered to send García Márquez to Europe as a foreign correspondant. The chaos and violence of Colombian politics made it impossible for him to write freely at home, and he was anxious to go. After covering a political conference in Geneva, he sent editorials and film reviews from Rome. Later, he visited and wrote essays about the socialist countries of eastern Europe. They were published in book form in 1978, with the title *De viaje por los países socialistas: 90 días en la "Cortina de Hierro"* ("Travelling in the Socialist Countries: 90 Days Behind the 'Iron Curtain'").

García Márquez was in Paris in 1956 when he read in a French newspaper that *El Espectador* had been closed down by the Colombian dictatorship. Although he had little money to live on, he chose to remain in Paris and concentrate on his fiction. In a tiny room that the hotel owner gave him for free, he worked on his novel *El Colonel no tiene quien le escriba* (*No One Writes to the Colonel*), about a retired colonel who waits patiently for his government pension in a decaying Colombian town. García Márquez claims to have rewritten this novel 11 times while living on chicken and watery soup.

The Colombian political situation was still chaotic in 1958. When a friend of García Márquez's offered him a job at a Venezuelan newspaper called *El Momento*, he accepted. During that year he wrote most of the stories that later appeared in *Los funerals de la Mamá Grande* (*Big Mama's Funeral*). He returned briefly to Colombia to marry his longtime girlfriend, Mercedes Barcha, to whom he had first proposed at age 13 while living with his family in Sucre.

The year 1959 was important for many Latin Americans: Fidel Castro led and won a revolution against a cruel dictator in Cuba. Latin Americans living in similar dictatorships became hopeful for their own futures. Many writers, including García Márquez, were enthusiastic about Castro and traveled to Cuba to offer their assistance. In 1959 García Márquez worked for Cuba's news agency, Prensa Latina, in Bogotá and in Cuba, and in 1960 he was sent to manage its office in New York City. The United States had supported the Cuban government at first, but when Castro became openly Communist, relations broke down. The news agency was closed in 1961, and García Márquez was once again out of a job. With a small loan from friends, he traveled to Mexico City by bus with his wife and young son Rodrigo, where he wrote for various newspapers and experimented with film. He collaborated on several screenplays with Carlos Fuentes. In 1961, he published *No One Writes to the Colonel*, followed by *Big Mama's Funeral*, the short-story collection, in 1962. They are considered to be the beginning of his best work.

The setting of these works is an isolated Colombian village, similar to that of his earlier stories. García Márquez's themes are social injustice, poverty and political corruption, which are reflected in the decaying tropical landscape and oppressive heat. The author's style in most of these stories was still fairly realistic and direct, but one story, "Big Mama's Funeral," was different from anything he had written before. The town of Macondo became the scene of magical and fantastic events only hinted at earlier. Magic and humor make their first appearance:

> This is, for all the world's unbelievers, the true account of Big Mama, absolute sovereign of the Kingdom of Macondo, who lived for ninety-two years, and died in the odor of sanctity one Tuesday last September and whose funeral was attended by the Pope.

Along with the pope, the president and other dignitaries, several dead people appear at Big Mama's funeral. No one is surprised to see them. The atmosphere is more like that of a circus or carnival than a funeral. In this story, García Márquez created a humorous satire of the church, government and political power through the use of exaggeration.

Following the publication of these two books, García Márquez experienced a period of writer's block. He simply did not feel inspired. But one day in 1965 he had a sudden vision while driving on a Mexican highway—the entire plot of *One Hundred Years of Solitude* came to him in a flash, and he made a U-turn and hurried home to write. After 18 months of daily writing, he mailed the manuscript to a publisher in Argentina. He sent it in several parts because he couldn't afford the postage required to send it all at once.

When *One Hundred Years of Solitude* was published in 1967, it was an instant success. It won several international literary prizes, including the Rómulo Gallegos prize (Venezuela) for the best Latin American novel in five years, in 1971. The English-language translation became a best-seller in the United States by 1970. Today it is available around the world in more than 30 languages.

Like the adventure stories García Márquez read in his youth, *One Hundred Years of Solitude* is a mixture of historical fact and fiction. It is the story of many generations of the Buendía family, but at the same time is also the history of Colombia and Latin America. It includes real wars, massacres, scientific inventions and natural disasters. A family tree at the beginning of the novel helps to distinguish among many characters with the same family names. The setting is Macondo; some of the characters resemble García Márquez's grandparents and other relatives. The novel's opening sentence recalls an incident from his childhood:

> Many years later, as he faced the firing squad, Colonel Aureliano Buendía was to remember that distant afternoon when his father took him to discover ice.

The great invention of *One Hundred Years of Solitude* is magical realism, a style that mixes magic or fantasy with detailed, everyday reality. Although fantastic events had occurred in literature before, they were usually found in myths and fairy tales written for children. But García Márquez began to use fantasy in a different way: He blended it with ordinary events in order to create a new kind of realism.

Upon the death of character José Arcadio Buendía, respected founder of the town of Macondo,

> . . . they saw a light rain of tiny yellow flowers falling. They fell on the town all through the night in a silent storm, and they covered the roofs and blocked the doors and smothered the animals who slept outdoors. So many flowers fell from the sky that in the morning the streets were carpeted with a compact cushion and they had to clear them away with shovels and rakes so that the funeral procession could pass by.

These events would be gruesome or frightening in other types of fiction. Here they are magical, beautiful and often comical, describing familiar situations in new ways.

García Márquez insists that he invents nothing, that his fiction is based on real—or what people believe to be real—events: In tropical regions of Latin America, rainstorms can last for days or even weeks; invasions of butterflies, birds and toads have been known to occur during extreme weather. The source of many of these images can be found in the tales he heard from his grandmother as a child.

Following the success of *One Hundred Years of Solitude*, García Márquez moved to Barcelona, Spain, in 1967 with his wife and two sons, hoping to find some solitude of his own and work on his next novel. Barcelona was popular with other Latin American writers at the time, many of them exiles from military governments. There he became friends with the Peruvian writer Mario Vargas Llosa, who published an admiring study of his work in 1971. García Márquez continued to write political and literary essays for newspapers and began a novel he had been planning for many years. *El otoño del patriarca* (*The Autumn of the Patriarch*), an ambitious and experimental work that explores of the mind of a tyrannical Latin American dictator, was published in 1975.

In 1975 García Márquez returned to Mexico City with his family, where he bought a house. Mexico had become a safer place than Colombia for him to live and to express himself freely. Since then, he has used his fame and economic security to support the international political causes he believes in: he has spoken and traveled on behalf of the Nicaraguan Revolution, worked to gain the release of political prisoners in Cuba and mediated between the Colombian government and guerrilla groups. He continues to write newspaper pieces on topics that are important to him.

In 1981, he published *Chronicle of a Death Foretold*, a short novel recounting the day of a murder. It is deceptively simple—at once a detective story, a love story, a fairy tale and a tragedy. The title word *Chronicle* recalls a form of newspaper account: Most of the dialogues are interviews with witnesses of a sensational murder in a small Caribbean town. In the novel, a young woman is married by her family to a wealthy, handsome and princelike stranger. When he discovers that she is not a virgin, he returns her to her home, and her brothers set out to kill the man they believe to be her

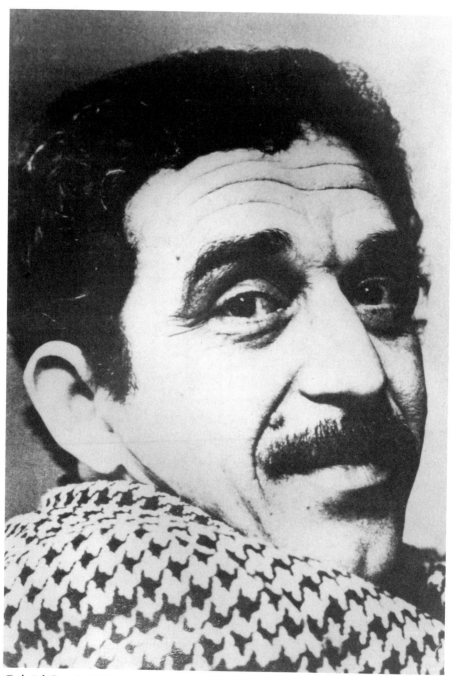

Gabriel García Márquez (Courtesy Columbus Memorial Library, Organization of American States)

lover. The time period is the 1920s, and the themes are the old-fashioned codes of honor and revenge.

In 1982 García Márquez was awarded the Nobel Prize in literature. The many public appearances and interviews that followed left him little time for writing. Again seeking solitude, he temporarily moved back to Cartagena de Indias, Colombia, to finish his next novel. *El amor en los tiempos del cólera* (*Love in the Time of Cholera*) was finally published toward the end of 1985 and became a best-seller throughout Latin America; when the English translation appeared in 1988, it was also a great success.

Love in the Time of Cholera is a love story, full of humor, warmth and wisdom. Like many of García Márquez's works, it takes place in the past and in the Caribbean region of Colombia. The story was inspired by the courtship between the author's parents in the 1920s: Like his father, the main character is a telegraph operator who falls in love with the daughter of an old and respectable family. Her father opposes the marriage and the couple is separated, although eventually reunited.

Love in the Time of Cholera is the author's most optimistic and humorous work. He uses irony to lighten what could have been a merely sentimental love story. The novel celebrates the wisdom of old age as well as the survival of love.

In recent years, García Márquez has resumed his involvement with film. In addition to work for the Cuban state film school, he wrote several screenplays for Spanish television, including *A Very Old Man*

"... There is no profession more solitary than that of the writer, in the sense that at the moment of writing nobody can help you, and nobody can know what it is that you want to do. No: you are alone, with an absolute solitude, face to face with a blank page."

with Enormous Wings and *Eréndira.* In 1989, he published a short novel called *El general en su laberinto* (*The General in His Labyrinth*), based on the life of Simon Bolívar, a hero who freed several South American countries from Spanish rule. *Doce cuentos peregrinos* (*Twelve Peregrine Tales*), published in 1992, is popular in both the English and Spanish versions.

In 1994, García Márquez's novel *Del amor y otros demonios* (*Of Love and Other Demons*) narrated the tragic fate of a young girl in 18th-century Colombia. The story was inspired by an incident from his reporting days in Cartagena in 1949. One day while searching for a story, he visited an old chapel that was being torn down. As the workers hastily pulled the old bones from their stone crypts, they discovered a long mane of golden hair attached to a small girl's skull. García Márquez was overcome with curiosity about the unknown girl and remembered a story his grandmother had told him long ago about a long-haired miracle worker. In his writer's mind, the two became one and resulted in this imaginative novel.

García Márquez is an immensely popular writer in Latin America and throughout the world. His aim is to tell good stories and to entertain, much in the way his grandmother once did. Macondo and its inhabitants are familiar to many Colombians and other Latin Americans, who can identify with its personalities, historical events and extreme weather conditions. But there is also a universal quality to his fiction that makes it readable and enjoyable for people everywhere.

Magical realism has appeared in the works of other Latin American writers—Juan Rulfo, Jorge Luis Borges, and Carlos Fuentes, among others—but García Márquez made it popular. He has a great ability to combine creative techniques with deep social concerns and, at the same time, be entertaining and humorous. His enormous success as a writer has drawn the attention of readers throughout the world to the rich and imaginative literature of Latin America.

Chronology

March 6, 1927 or 1928	Gabriel José García Márquez born in Aracataca, Colombia
1955	Publishes *Leafstorm*, first novel
1958	Marries Mercedes Barcha
1961	Publishes *No One Writes to the Colonel* and *Big Mama's Funeral*
1967	*One Hundred Years of Solitude*, novel
1975	Publishes *The Autumn of the Patriarch*
1981	*Chronicle of a Death Foretold*, novel
1982	Awarded the Nobel Prize in literature
1985	*Love in the Time of Cholera*, novel
1994	*Of Love and Other Demons*, novel

Further Reading

GARCÍA MÁRQUEZ'S WORKS

Chronicle of a Death Foretold. Translated from the Spanish by Gregory Rabassa. New York: Knopf, 1983.

Love in the Time of Cholera. Translated from the Spanish by Edith Grossman. New York: Knopf, 1988.

Of Love and Other Demons. Translated from the Spanish by Edith Grossman. New York: Knopf, 1995.

One Hundred Years of Solitude. Translated from the Spanish by Gregory Rabassa. London: Jonathan Cape, 1991.

BOOKS ABOUT GABRIEL GARCÍA MÁRQUEZ

Raymond L. Williams. *Gabriel García Márquez*. Twayne's World Authors Series, 749 (Latin American Authors). Boston: Twayne Publishers, 1984. Good study of author's life and major work.

Jorge Amado in Paris in 1992 (Zélia Gattai)

Jorge Amado

MAGICIAN OF BAHIA (1912–)

When Jorge Amado was less than a year old, his father was shot and wounded before his eyes. Born in 1912 in northeast Brazil, the author was witness to a violent period in the region's history. Desperate frontier dwellers fought and killed for precious farmland, where they hoped to make their fortunes on vast plantations.

Amado grew up amid poverty as well as violence. He watched as farmworkers were mistreated and underpaid by wealthy landowners. As a youth, he became concerned with the injustices suffered by the poor; as he matured, he wrote about them. His long career as a journalist, politician and novelist all had the goal of achieving justice and freedom for the poor and marginalized people of Brazil. Of all his life's work, his novels have reached the largest audience; but while addressing his country's social problems, they also celebrate the warmth and humanity of Brazil and its people. His works are well loved in Brazil and abroad for their realism as well as their humor, fun and magic.

Brazil is the largest country in Latin America and is very different from its neighbors. While Spain had colonized most of the surrounding countries, Brazil had been claimed by Portugal. Beginning in the year 1500, Portuguese explorers began to settle in what is now the state of Bahia in northeast Brazil. During the 16th and 17th centuries, they brought slaves from the African countries across the Atlantic to use as laborers on vast sugar and coffee plantations. The white Portuguese mixed freely with black Africans and with the local Indians, creating a nation of many colors. Although Portuguese is still Brazil's official language, her people are African, Indian and European.

Bahia was the site of Brazil's first city. For 200 years, Salvador (formerly São Salvador) was the Brazilian capital and the center of Portugal's far-flung empire. The Portuguese who settled there were Catholic, like their Spanish neighbors, but the long years of slave trade changed Bahia's culture and soul: The religion, food, music and dance of the entire region are more African than Portuguese. Jorge Amado spent his childhood there, and returned to live there later in life after many years' absence. He has always called Bahia home, and it is an enduring presence in his fiction.

Jorge Amado's parents, João Amado de Faria and Eulália Leal, immigrated to Bahia from the inland state of Sergipe. Like thousands of others, they journeyed there in the early 1900s to clear the jungle and plant cacao. Cacao beans, from which chocolate is made, grow at the end of a round, golden fruit. Because of the fruit's color, this rush for land has often been compared to the gold rush in California and Alaska. Like panning for gold, cacao harvesting was often a dangerous occupation. Rival planters fought and killed one another for the valuable land.

Amado was born at the family's cacao farm, Auricídia, in Ferradas, southern Bahia. His childhood years were marked by the violence of the "cacao wars" as well as natural disasters. In his 1981 memoir, *O menino grapiuna* (Boy from southern Bahia), he recounted his father's ambush in 1913:

From my mother's telling it so many times, the scene
became as vivid and real to me as if I had actually
retained some memory of it. . . . Ten months old, I was
crawling on the farmhouse veranda toward the end of
sunset. . . . My father was cutting some cane for the
mare, his favorite mount. The gunman, hiding behind a
guava tree, rested his repeater in the fork of its branches
. . . awaiting the right moment to fire it. . . . The animal
caught the fatal bullet, [but] pieces of lead embedded in
[Father's] shoulders and back. . . . [He] was just able to
pick up his son and carry him into the kitchen, where
Doña Eulália was fixing dinner. He handed her the boy
all covered with his father's blood.

His father survived the attack, but further misfortunes
soon befell the Amado family. The Cachoeira River over-
flowed its banks the following year, destroying the family
farm. Soon after, a smallpox epidemic broke out, leaving
members of almost every local family dead. The Amados
found shelter in the seaport town of Ilhéus, where they began
to scrape together a living selling sandals. By 1917, they had
saved enough money to buy another plot of land in the
country, and moved into a new farmhouse. The cacao wars
continued, and Jorge watched in fear as his father led groups
of gunmen into the night. Lasting images from stories Amado
heard as a child were later woven into several of his novels.

By 1918 the Amados had become more prosperous, and
they bought a second home in Ilhéus. Six-year-old Jorge
Amado was sent there to the grammar school of Doña
Guilhermina, a strict disciplinarian who would later appear in
his novels Terras do sem fim (The Violent Land) and Gabriela.
Amado's three brothers—Jofre, Joelson and James—were born
in 1918, 1920 and 1922 respectively. Jofre, however, died at the
age of three in 1921.

When Amado was 10, he was sent to the Antonio Vieira
School in Salvador, the state capital. It was a prestigious

Catholic boarding school, and Jorge was introduced to Portuguese and English literature. His teacher read one of his essays aloud in writing class, declaring that one day he would be a writer. But life at school was too strict for Amado, who had grown up wild and free in the country, and he fell into a depression.

At the age of 12, Amado ran away when his father refused to transfer him to another school. Alone and penniless, he wandered through the desolate backlands of Bahia, where he came into contact with a wide variety of people, most of whom were very poor. In a 1990 interview, the author recalled:

> I ran away from school, and headed toward the interior of the state, the backlands. I traveled any way I could, by train, by boat, on foot, on horseback. It was an unhurried journey. . . . My money ran out, but I didn't need it any more. I went on, always finding people who gave me things, helped me, and that was so great. There I had my first contact with freedom, with people of all kinds, from farmers to the poorest people imaginable, I slept in I don't know how many houses, I ate at I don't know how many tables of many families, until I arrived at my grandfather's house, in Itaporanga.

He was deeply impressed by the generosity and warmth of these people who had so little, yet gave him food and shelter. They would later become the subject of not only his fiction as well as his entire life's work. His journey ended two months later at his grandfather's home in distant Sergipe.

Amado expected his father to be angry when he finally returned home. Instead, he was calmly told that if he didn't want to study, he could work on the family farm. After six months, however, he went back to Salvador, this time to the Colégio Iparinga, another private but more liberal school that suited his lively character better. He remembers climbing the walls each night to escape to adventure in the streets below.

Amado began to write while still a young teenager, and at 13 he became director of his school newspaper. Soon after, he founded a student literary journal called *A Folha* (The paper), where he published his first stories and articles. In 1927, when he was only 15, Amado left school and began to work for the city newspaper, *Diário do Bahia*. At first, his job was only to compile police reports, but when the paper's editor saw an article he had written about the violence in the cacao region, he was impressed and promoted the young man to reporter. It was the beginning of a long career in journalism.

From a young age, Amado showed signs of rebellion. He hated school because of the discipline it required; yet he was intellectually curious. He loved to read and preferred to learn from books rather than from teachers in classrooms. His entire life has been a struggle against convention, conformity and mediocrity. It was Amado's search for freedom of life-style and of expression that led him to become a writer.

Amado began to publish stories, poems and essays in newspapers and in such literary journals as the short-lived *Meridiano* and *A Semana*, published by a group of young writers and poets called the "Academy of Rebels." These writers gathered around the poet Pinheiro Viegas and were influenced by the Modernist literary movement that had begun in Rio a few years earlier. Like the Ultraists in Argentina, such as Jorge Luis Borges and his friends, their aim was to revitalize literature by creating radically new styles. Some of these writers became Amado's lifelong friends. His first novel, *Land of Carnival* (1931), was based on these years.

Amado's family was no longer poor and had high but conventional expectations of their eldest son. But instead of becoming a lawyer or businessman, he chose to live on his own small salary from the newspaper, and in 1928 moved to the Pelourinho, then a slum district in the oldest part of Salvador. It was a picturesque but rundown area, home to Afro-Brazilians, cult worshipers and struggling artists. Amado identified strongly with these people and was fascinated with their Afro-Brazilian religion, *candomblé* or *macumba*, which fuses the worship of Catholic saints with African gods in a powerful and surreal way. Amado's experiences there would form the background of several of his novels, including *Jubiabá* and *Doña Flor e seus dois maridos* (*Doña Flor and Her Two Husbands*).

In 1930, Amado moved to Rio de Janeiro. His father had encouraged him to study law, and after taking some preparatory courses he enrolled in the National Law School in 1931. But he always preferred literature and history to law. He claims to have never opened a law book, and quickly became involved with Rio's young writers and artists. That same year, he published his first novel, *O país do carnaval* (*Land of Carnival*). He was only 19 years old.

Land of Carnival, a witty novel about a group of young Brazilian writers and intellectuals, much like the Academy of Rebels, was a minor success among other writers. While continuing his law studies (he received his diploma in 1935), Amado energetically produced several more novels in quick succession. In 1933, he married Matilde García Rosa. They had a daughter, Lila, in 1935, who died suddenly while Amado was living abroad in 1949.

In the 1930s, Brazilian writers were united in their fight against social injustice. Their novels and stories, written in a style called social realism, described the hardships of Brazil's poor and pressed for changes in government and society. Amado's early novels were powerful examples of this style.

In *Cacau* (1933) and *Jubiabá* (1935), he wrote about the mistreatment of black and mestizo laborers in his native Bahia; the prostitutes and dockworkers of Salvador are the subjects of *Suor* (*Sweat*, 1934); *Mar morto* (*Sea of Death*, 1936) describes the plight of Bahia's fishers; and *Capitães da areia* (*Captains of the Sand*, 1937) is about the tragic lives of street children. These novels are full of the violence, epidemics, floods and droughts that Amado knew from childhood. All protest strongly against injustice and racism.

Amado quickly became famous for the important themes of these early novels, but he also came to the attention of the Brazilian government, which was ruled by the dictator Getúlio Vargas during much of his lifetime. The Vargas government severely repressed all forms of social protest and, beginning in 1936, Amado was jailed on several occasions for his writing and political activities. He spent many years of his life in exile, and his books were often censored. In 1937, 2,000 copies of *Captains of the Sand* were burned in a public plaza by the military.

Although these early novels were powerful and serious, they were not very sophisticated. Most of them had simple plots and repetitive themes; the language was realistic, direct and full of slang; his characters were either good and poor or evil and rich, with little variation. Amado was criticized by some intellectuals for using his novels to advance his own leftist political beliefs.

But there were signs of promise in these early novels; *Jubiabá* is considered the best of them. It concerns an orphaned black boy who becomes a beggar and delinquent but turns his life around as he learns about the history and culture of his people. The

"I have always sought the uncomfortable road of commitment to the poor and the oppressed, to those who have nothing, who struggle for a place in the sun . . . and I have tried to be, insofar as I could, a voice for their longings, sorrows, and hopes. . . ."

novel has the lyrical descriptions of Afro-Brazilian folk customs and religious rites that characterize some of Amado's later novels.

Amado was jailed briefly in 1936 for allegedly supporting an uprising against the Vargas government. In 1937, he traveled to several Latin American countries, where he met some of his favorite artists and writers, including the Mexican painter Diego Rivera and the Chilean poet Pablo Neruda. When he returned to Brazil, the worst period of repression by the Vargas dictatorship was just beginning. Amado was jailed in the Amazon city of Manaus, and his books were banned and burned throughout Brazil.

When he was released from prison in 1938, Amado spent several months in the city of São Paulo, and then in Estância, in the state of Sergipe. He wrote little during this period, probably due to the harsh political climate, but he did publish a book of poems called *A estrada do mar* (Star of the Sea). In 1939, he moved to Rio in an attempt to pursue his literary activities, but was discouraged by the lack of freedom of expression and in 1941 moved to Argentina.

During the next two years, Amado published biographies of two Brazilian literary and political figures. He also collaborated on a collective novel called *Brandão entre o mar e o amor* (Brandão between the sea and love) with the writers Graciliano Ramos, José Lins do Rêgo, Rachel de Queiroz and Aníbal Machado.

Amado spent several periods of time away from Brazil during his lifetime, either willingly or under protest, but he always felt the need to return, even when conditions were dangerous. In 1942, he returned again, only to be immediately jailed in Rio. He was released a few months later, on the condition that he remain in the city of Salvador. In 1943, he covered the daily events of World War II for the Bahian newspaper *O Imparcial* and continued an aggressive campaign in the press for a return to democracy and increased freedom of expression.

In 1943, Amado's novel *The Violent Land*, which he had written mostly while living in Argentina, was published to great acclaim. Many critics consider it to be Amado's masterpiece. An epic frontier tale, it tells of land battles between two powerful estates for the last cacao groves in Bahia. Although the region prospers, it is at the cost of moral values and human lives. Taking place around the time of Amado's birth, the novel is full of childhood memories and stories told to him by relatives. His language is more poetic than in his earlier works, and a kind of ironic humor begins to appear.

In 1945, the First Congress of Brazilian Writers was held in São Paulo, and Amado was elected its vice president. The meeting was as political as it was literary, for the important writers and intellectuals who attended were members of communist and social democratic groups. They were united in protest of the Vargas dictatorship, which was slowly coming to an end. It was there that Amado met Zélia Gattai, a young writer who admired his work immensely and shared his political concerns. One day, not long after their first meeting, he asked her to read his daily column in the newspaper *Folha da Manha*. It was a passionate declaration of love, addressed to Zélia and began "To you I will give the sky and the sea. . . ."

Amado had been legally separated from his first wife in 1944 after years of physical separation due to exile and prison. Divorce, however, was illegal in Brazil at the time, and so he asked Zélia to "marry" him without a ceremony. They began their life together in São Paulo in 1945. In 1978, they were formally married.

The Vargas dictatorship came to an end in 1945, but Amado continued to be active in politics and was elected an official of the Brazilian Communist Party in 1946. He worked hard to pass laws to protect all kinds of freedom of expression and helped to draft the new Brazilian constitution of 1946, which he also signed. He and Zélia traveled throughout Brazil while he campaigned for the party and gave impassioned speeches. Although he had little time for writing, he published another successful novel, *Red Harvest*, in 1946 about the lives of a migrant-laboring family. Their first child, Jorge João, was born in 1947.

The political situation took a turn for the worse in 1948 when the Communist Party was outlawed and its members' lives put at risk. Amado and his family left Brazil for voluntary exile in Europe. They spent two years in Paris, where they made friends among important writers and artists of the time, including Jean-Paul Sartre, Simone de Beauvoir, Paul Eluard and Pablo Picasso. He visited Poland as vice president of the World Congress of Writers and Artists for Peace and traveled widely with his family in Asia and the Soviet Union. They were living in Prague, Czechoslovakia, when their daughter Paloma was born in 1951.

The Amados returned to Brazil in 1952 and set up residence in Rio de Janeiro. Amado had come to believe that unless he gave up politics, his writing career would be finished; he realized that his novels would reach and influence many more people than his speeches ever could. He also became disillusioned with communism during the 1950s, when writers were censored and imprisoned in the Soviet Union. He formally left the Communist Party in 1955. Although he continued to speak out against repression everywhere, he began to devote more time to his writing. His fiction changed dramatically after this— many believed for the better.

In 1958, Amado published *Gabriela, cravo e canela* (*Gabriela, Clove and Cinnamon*), which was an immediate success, winning five major literary prizes and later becoming a best-seller in the United States. In this novel, Amado continues to describe Brazilian society, culture and politics, but he does so with poetry, fun and good humor. This was the "new" Jorge Amado.

The novel has comic section and chapter headings that are long and wordy, imitating the chronicles of early explorers:

> PART ONE. Adventures and misadventures of a good Brazilian (born in Syria), all in the town of Ilhéus in 1925, when cacao flourished and progress reigned, with love affairs, murders, banquets, creches, divers stories for all tastes. . . .

The town of Ilhéus in southern Bahia is once again the setting. But the wars of the frontier are over, and the towns-people are prosperous and "civilized." When Gabriela, a young and lively immigrant from the interior arrives, she liberates the town from the old-fashioned, chauvinistic values of the wealthy local landowners. It is clear that Amado is still concerned with the Bahian poor. But this time love and humor, instead of bloodshed and violence, are the instruments of change and justice.

A morte e a morte de Quincas Berro Dágua (*The Two Deaths of Quincas Wateryell*, 1959) and *A completa verdade sobre as discutidas aventuras do Comandante Vasco Moscoso de Argão, capitõ de longo curso* (*Home Is the Sailor*, 1961) are good examples of Amado's new style, being tall tales about men who find happiness living outrageous, unconventional lives that make respectable society seem hollow and absurd. These stories concern the relativity of truth and make use of multiple points of view and other innova-

"I couldn't have written about Bahia, pretended to be a novelist of Bahia, if I hadn't really known the *candomblés* from the inside, as I do, which is the religion of the people of Bahia."

tions. Amado's writing was beginning to show some of the dazzling new techniques that were appearing in other experimental Latin American novels of the time. His use of humor and magic is more closely linked to the work of Gabriel García Márquez than to that of other writers of the "boom." In 1961, Amado was elected to the prestigious Brazilian Academy of Letters.

The best-loved of all Amado's novels, *Doña Flor and Her Two Husbands*, was published in 1966. It is a comic, magical tale about Bahia in the 1920s and 1930s. Flor, a respectable woman who gives cooking classes in her home in Salvador, is married to Vadinho, who is wild, fun-loving and irresponsible. She complains when he gambles and womanizes, but loves him passionately, forgiving him again and again. Amado criticizes Vadinho's unconventionality with the same loving affection he showed for Quincas and other characters.

The opening pages contain quotes by the novel's characters and even a letter from Doña Flor to the author. Her recipes for delicious Bahian dishes introduce many chapters. The author's real-life friends appear in the story and play the music called for in the chapter headings. The Afro-Bahian religion, *candomblé*, plays an important part in the novel. Amado knows this spiritual world well and is himself an official of a cult in Salvador. During elaborate ceremonies, African gods of the waters or of war are called to life. Women dance to the sound of drums until they feel they are possessed by Yemanja, Oxossi, Xango or Exu.

Many of Amado's readers were surprised at the pure fun of this novel. But some choose to see Flor as a symbol of Brazil and her husbands as rival political ideologies. Neither Flor nor Brazil can live without both passion and intelligence, heart and mind. *Doña Flor* was made into a popular film in 1976.

Amado and his family had returned to live in Salvador in 1963. His most popular novels take place there, and many

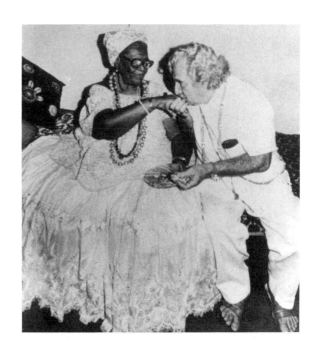

Jorge Amado asking the blessing of a high priestess of candomblé *(Zélia Gattai)*

local people appear in their pages. He is a well-known and loved figure there—he has dozens of godchildren, and restaurants and cafes are named after people and places in his books.

In 1964, a new military dictatorship began in Brazil. It lasted more than 20 years, ending in 1985. Although Amado did not experience the persecution he had in earlier years, there was great social unrest in Brazil. He continued his fights against censorship and refused to submit any of his novels to the official government censor. During the 1970s, Amado traveled with his family to Europe, Canada and the United States, visiting friends and writing. He spent several months as as writer-in-residence at Pennsylvania State University in 1971, working on his novel *Tereza Batista, cansada de guerra* (*Tereza Batista: Home from the Wars*), a strange mixture of realism, magic and comedy. Amado, his friends and family appear throughout and are guests at the main character's wedding. Multiple narrators interrupt with rumors and tales of Tereza, as if she were real, but werewolves, headless mules and other fantastic creatures appear. Superstition, voodoo and Afro-Brazilian gods play important roles.

Three of Amado's novels were made into films in Brazil in the 1970s, and several others became television soap operas. Amado became so popular that he had little time for what he does best—writing. In 1976 and 1977, he escaped to London to work on his next novel, *Tieta do Agreste, pastora de cabras* (*Tieta the Goat Girl*, 1979), another comic novel about a poor country girl who becomes successful through unusual means.

Amado's later novels are comic, magical and entertaining. He is a master at weaving together dozens of separate plots in one book. Although still critical of the government and of social conventions, he uses inventive new techniques in his tales: Satire and irony take the place of political propaganda, and they have colorful, often circuslike atmospheres. While he makes fun of all his characters, Amado's heroes and heroines are still the poor and uneducated. In recent years, critics have attacked these novels, claiming they romanticize the poor; some accuse him of merely imitating popular literature in order to appeal to the masses.

"My literature and my life have one characteristic trait in common: never to depart from the life and the concerns of my Brazilian people."

Controversy has always surrounded Amado's work. The Brazilian government, as well as literary critics, have often reacted strongly to it: Until the 1950s, his novels were censored, and he suffered prison or exile because of their content. Literary critics have called Amado's novels too realistic or too romantic, too serious or too entertaining, too truthful and too poetic—perhaps because Amado has been writing for so many years and literary styles fall in and out of fashion. But Amado has always written exactly what he wanted to write.

In 1981, Jorge Amado celebrated his 50th year as a novelist. That same year, he published *O menino grapiuna*, a memoir of his childhood in southern Bahia. Many memorable scenes, events and characters from his novels can be found in its pages. Amado's wife, Zélia Gattai, has also published three books of memoirs about her life with Amado; unfortunately, none of these are as yet available in English.

Among Amado's latest novels are *Tocaia grande* (*Show Down*, 1984), a historical frontier tale about his native Bahia, and *Sumiço da santa* (*The War of the Saints*, 1988), in which a statue of the Catholic St. Barbara comes to life and is transformed into the African goddess St. Barbara Yansan. It is another amusing tale about Amado's beloved Bahia, as always fondly critical of all members of its diverse society.

In his long lifetime, Jorge Amado has published 32 books that have been translated into 48 languages. He will soon appear in *The Guinness Book of World Records* as the world's most frequently translated author. In 1995, new revised editions of many of his works began to appear. They are being revised by the author's favorite critic, his daughter Paloma. When asked when his next book will arrive, he complains that phone calls, faxes and visits from his friends and fans keep him from his favorite activity—writing.

Chronology

August 10, 1912	Jorge Amado born in southern Bahia
1913	Father wounded in ambush
1914	Family moves to Ilhéus
1918–25	Attends school in Ilhéus and Salvador; runs away in 1924

1927	Reporter for *Diário da Bahia*
1930	Moves to Rio de Janeiro; Getúlio Vargas takes power
1931	Begins law school; publishes first novel, *Land of Carnival*
1933	Publishes *Cacao*; marries Matilde García Rosa
1935	Finishes law school; daughter Lila born; *Jubiabá* published
1936	Jailed in Rio by Vargas government; *Sea of Death*
1937	Copies of *Captains of the Sands* burned; travels throughout Latin America; jailed in Manaus
1941	Exile in Argentina
1943	*The Violent Land*
1944	Separated from first wife
1945	Meets Zélia Gattai, his second wife; elected deputy of the Brazilian Communist Party
1947	Son Jorge born
1948	Communist Party outlawed; exile in Europe
1949	Daughter Lila dies in Rio
1951	Daughter Paloma born in Czechoslovakia
1952	Family returns to live in Brazil
1958	*Gabriela* published; wins 5 major prizes
1959	*The Two Deaths of Quincas Wateryell*
1961	Elected to Brazilian Academy of Letters; *Home Is the Sailor*
1963	Family takes up residence in Salvador, Bahia
1964	Military dictatorship takes over in Brazil
1966	*Doña Flor and Her Two Husbands*

1971	Travels to the United States and Canada; *Tereza Batista: Home from the Wars*
1976	Lives in London; film version of *Doña Flor*
1978	Officially marries Zélia Gattai
1979	*Tieta the Goat Girl*
1981	*O menino grapiuna* (childhood memoirs)
1984	*Show Down*
1985	Return of civilian government in Brazil
1988	*The War of the Saints*

Further Reading

AMADO'S WORKS

Doña Flor and Her Two Husbands: A Moral and Amorous Tale. Translated by Harriet de Onis. New York: Avon, 1988.

Gabriela, Clove and Cinnamon. Translated by James L. Taylor and William Grossman. New York: Knopf, 1962.

Show Down. Translated by Gregory Rabassa. New York: Bantam, 1988.

The Two Deaths of Quincas Wateryell. Translated by Barbara Shelby. New York: Knopf, 1965.

The Violent Land. Translated by Samuel Putnam. New York: Knopf, 1945.

The War of the Saints. Translated by Gregory Rabassa. New York: Bantam, 1993.

BOOKS ABOUT JORGE AMADO

Bobby J. Chamberlain. *Jorge Amado.* Twayne's World Authors Series, Latin American Literature (767). Boston: Twayne Publishers, 1990. Good study of author's life and major works through 1988.

Fred P. Ellison. *Brazil's New Novel: Four Northeastern Masters.* Berkeley: University of California Press, 1954. Includes studies of Amado's early works.

Carlos Fuentes

Carlos Fuentes

HISTORY AND IDENTITY (1928–   )

Carlos Fuentes has probably done more to teach the world about Latin America than any other writer of his time. His many novels, stories and plays explore the rich history and culture of Mexico, and his essays on Latin American politics and culture appear regularly in the world's most important newspapers and journals. Currently, he is a frequent and popular lecturer at American and European universities.

From a young age, Carlos Fuentes was well trained for this role of cultural ambassador. His father, Rafael Fuentes Boettiger, was a diplomat who moved frequently to occupy posts throughout Latin America; young Fuentes and his mother, Berta Macías, accompanied him. An only child, Fuentes was born in Panama City in 1928 and spent his first years in Quito, Montevideo and Rio de Janeiro, the capitals of Ecuador, Uruguay, and Brazil. When he was six, his father was appointed counselor to the Mexican Embassy in Washington, D.C. "During our family discussions at the dinner table, relations between Mexico and the United States were paramount," Fuentes remembered in a 1995 interview. In later years, they continued to be the subject of many of his political essays.

From 1934 to 1940, Fuentes attended the Henry Cooke Public School in Washington, which he described as "an American melting pot." He soon spoke more English than Spanish, even though he spent his summers in Mexico. Adapting well to life in Washington, he felt no different than the children in his classes who were born in the United States: He read Dick Tracy and Superman comic books, traded bubble-gum cards, and went to movie matinees on Saturdays (he is still a great fan of classic American movies). He began to feel that Mexico and the Spanish language were make-believe, like the bedtime stories his parents told him: "Mexico was an imaginary country," recalled Fuentes in a 1988 interview. "I thought my father had invented it to amuse me. It seemed so exotic, so different from where I was living."

But in 1938, an event occurred that reminded Carlos Fuentes of his true identity. Lázaro Cárdenas, the Mexican president, created an international scandal by suddenly nationalizing the country's oil resources. This meant that U.S. oil companies were taken over by the Mexican government and that American workers lost their jobs. Newspaper headlines attacked "red" and "communist" Mexico, calling for invasion and boycott; Fuentes was singled out at school as a Mexican, a foreigner and an enemy.

In 1941, Fuentes's father was transferred to South America once again. The family lived in Chile for a time, and later in Argentina. It was

> "In Chile I came to know the possibilities of our language for giving wing to freedom and poetry. The impression was enduring; it links me forever to that sad and wonderful land. It lives within me, and it transformed me into a man who knows how to dream, love, insult, and write only in Spanish."

in Chile, a country renowned for poets, that the young man came to love the Spanish language. He has a vivid memory of hearing coal miners sing verses of Pablo Neruda's poems on a southern beach. It was then that he realized that Spanish was a real and living language, not just his parents' private code. He began to read all the books in Spanish he could find.

Fuentes was 16 years old when his family finally returned to live in Mexico City in 1944; by then, his Spanish accent and vocabulary were more South American than Mexican. He had to work hard to learn his own Mexican Spanish and culture, which were quite different. After completing his high school education at the private Colegio México in 1946, Fuentes attended the Colegio Francés Morelos, a French preparatory school, from 1947 to 1949.

When he returned to Mexico, Carlos Fuentes became obsessed with his Mexican identity and culture. Because Mexico was a foreign place for him, he approached it with the curiosity of an outsider. This objective vision of his native land and culture, combined with a great love and curiosity, underlies the best of Fuentes's later fiction.

Fuentes had been writing since his school days in Washington. His first "publication" was a personal magazine in English, written and illustrated by hand. It contained drawings, news items and book reviews, and each month's single copy was circulated to the neighbors in his apartment building.

Later, in Chile, he wrote an adventure novel that imitated such favorite French classics as *The Three Musketeers* and *The Count of Monte Cristo*. "It was a gothic melodrama, which began in Marseilles and ended on a hilltop in Haiti with a black tyrant whose mad French mistress is hidden in the attic." He now laughs fondly at how terrible it was. The only person he read it to—exiled Mexican artist David Alfaro Siqueiros—fell soundly asleep in a Chilean vineyard. There is no surviving copy. During those years, Fuentes also published some fantastic stories in the literary magazine of the Grange School, the private British school he attended. In Mexico, he continued to publish stories during his school years.

Fuentes prepared to follow in his father's diplomatic footsteps. In 1950, he spent a year in Switzerland, studying international law at the University of Geneva. While there, he served as a Mexican delegate to the International Labour Organisation. It was his first trip to Europe, and he took advantage of it to perfect his French and become more familiar with French literature, which he admired.

Upon his return to Mexico in 1951, Fuentes enrolled in the National University of Mexico to study law at his parents' insistence: "They told me to study law because I would die of hunger if I tried to live off my writing in Mexico," he recalled. He became secretary for cultural affairs at the university and, later, head of the Department for Cultural Relations at the Mexican Ministry of Foreign Affairs.

During the 1950s, Fuentes published a steady stream of articles on literature, the arts and politics in Mexican journals. He wrote for and edited the journal of the Universidad de México and in 1956 was a founding member of the *Revista Mexicana de Literatura*, a progressive literary journal that introduced new writing by international authors. It was one of the first to publish the innovative short stories of Julio Cortázar, Jorge Luis Borges and other new Latin American writers.

In 1954, Fuentes published his first short story collection, *Los días enmascarados* (The masked days). His first novel, *La región más transparente* (*Where the Air Is Clear*),

"When I finally arrived in Mexico, I discovered that my father's imaginary country was real, but more fantastic than any imaginary land."

appeared only four years later in 1958. It was widely read and caused a sensation in Mexico, and Fuentes quickly became known as the best young Mexican author of his time. Confident that he could make a living as a writer, he left his diplomatic career behind. He is the only writer of the Latin American "boom" generation to have supported himself by writing since his youth.

The literary climate in Mexico in the 1950s was similar to that in much of Latin America: Most fiction described local Mexican settings and traditional country life; realistic art and literature—especially that which praised the Mexican Revolution—were highly respected.

The Mexican Revolution (1910–20) was the most important event in 20th-century Mexican history. It began with the overthrow of the dictator Porfirio Díaz by armies of workers and peasants led by Emiliano Zapata and Pancho Villa. During years of violent clashes, land was seized from the rich and given to the poor; foreign businesses, styles and ideas, popular with the earlier government, were thrown out; and Mexican nationalism became the rule of the day.

For years afterward, literature and the arts reflected these changes. Such Mexican muralists as Diego Rivera painted colorful images that glorified the revolution and its heroes and romanticized Indians and mestizos in larger-than-life wall paintings. Novels such as Mariano Azuela's *The Underdogs* told of heroic struggles that led to the revolution's triumph. While much of this was good art, it soon became stale and official. When Carlos Fuentes began to write, Mexican literature was ready for a change.

Fuentes's stories and novels were different from just about anything published before in Mexico. He wrote about modern life in Mexico City, a setting seldom used in the past, but a profound sense of history pervades this modern life. Ancient Indian gods, myths and legends continue to haunt Fuentes's characters as they uselessly try to ignore or escape the weight of Mexico's past, be it ancient Indian or that of the more recent revolution.

The early stories of *Los días enmascarada* (The masked days) show Fuentes's concern with modern-day Mexico as well as its past. In style, they have elements of magical realism and fantasy, and like the stories of Julio Cortázar, whom Fuentes greatly admired, they describe the eruption of strange events into everyday life. In the story "Chac-Mool," the ancient Mayan rain god of that name comes to life in the moldy cellar of a Mexico City home. "In a Flemish Garden" tells of the haunting of an old Mexico City mansion by the Empress Carlota, wife of the French Emperor Maximilian who ruled Mexico from 1864 to 1867.

Fuentes's first novel, *Where the Air Is Clear*, is a critical portrait of Mexico City. The very title is ironic and comes from an early explorer's description of the volcano-encircled plateau where the city was built. By the 1950s, Mexico City was already on the way to becoming the world's largest city, barely visible in the smog created by industry and exhaust fumes.

Where the Air Is Clear is a chaotic, complex novel with nearly a hundred different characters from all levels of Mexican society, rich and poor, white, mestizo and Indian. The novel criticizes the failure of the revolution to resolve Mexico's deep social problems.

Ancient and modern ways of life in Mexico are contrasted in powerful images throughout the novel. The neon lights of the modern city are reminders of the power of the Aztec gods of fire and water. Symbols of the Aztec past appear amid the modern life of the city's central plaza, ". . . a corner where stone broke into shapes of flaming shafts and red skulls and still butterflies: a wall of snakes beneath the twin roofs of rain and fire."

Like other writers of the "boom" in Latin American literature, Fuentes experimented with new techniques: The

Carlos Fuentes   (Joe Wrinn; Courtesy of Harvard News Office)

plot of *Where the Air Is Clear*, as in much of his work, is fragmented; images are jumbled together, and events occur out of order; cinematic effects—flashbacks and rapid jumps between scenes—are used. While all these new techniques were new to Mexican writing, they were established elements of Fuentes's favorite European and North American novels. Interestingly, such writers as Mario Vargas Llosa and Julio Cortázar were experimenting with similar techniques at about the same time. The authors only met years later in Paris.

In 1959, Fuentes married Rita Macedo, a Mexican film actress. They shared an interest in film and theatre, which have always been subjects of Fuentes's journal articles. The couple had a daughter, Cecilia, in 1962 and moved to Paris together a few years later, but their marriage ended in divorce in 1969.

Fuentes became politically committed to Socialist ideas during the 1950s, as did many other intellectuals of the time. He believed that the enormous gulf between rich and poor in his country could be lessened by a radical sharing of wealth and property. In 1959, Fuentes was one of a group of intellectuals who were enthusiastic about the Communist Cuban revolution of Fidel Castro. Shortly after Castro's victory, Fuentes traveled with other writers to Cuba to show his support. He was a juror for Cuba's Casa de las América's literary award as were other prominent writers of the "boom," and throughout the 1950s and 1960s, his articles on politics appeared in the leftist Mexican journals *Siempre!* and *Política*.

During his visit to Cuba, Fuentes began to work on a novel, *La muerte de Artemio Cruz* (*The Death of Artemio Cruz*), his most popular—and generally believed to be his best—work. After its publication in Mexico in 1962 it was translated into 15 languages.

Fuentes's first novel is a portrait of Mexico City as seen through the lives of dozens of characters, but *The Death of Artemio Cruz* describes all of Mexico through the life of a single man. Again, Mexico's present and past are contrasted, but the Mexican Revolution rather than the Aztec past is the backdrop for *Artemio Cruz*.

The Death of Artemio Cruz takes place during the last 12 hours in the life of a wealthy old man who had been a hero in the Mexican Revolution. Lying on his deathbed, he relives vivid episodes from his long and eventful life, including violent battles of the revolution and the corruption of its goals in later years. It continues the author's criticism of Mexican society from a socialist viewpoint.

Fuentes developed a dazzling new technique in this novel: The character Artemio Cruz is the only narrator, but he has several different voices. As Cruz reviews his long life, he refers to himself as "I," "you" and "he." The "I" voice describes the present, his sick body lying in bed attended to by the priest, his wife and his daughter. In order to escape the horror of the present, he begins to recall his past. He calls himself "you" when contemplating the recent past of corrupt business dealings and politics. As he remembers his youth—the years during and after the revolution—Cruz thinks of himself as "he" or "Artemio Cruz." He also uses different tenses, or times: "I am," "you will be" and "he was" mix together on the same page.

This technique, which shows the complex and divided personality of Artemio Cruz, also mirrors the deep contradictions in Mexican society and history. Through the life of one man, a portrait of a tragic life, a troubled country and a violent history emerges.

Carlos Fuentes refuses to be categorized. Although the themes of Mexican history and identity continually appear in his fiction, he has frequently changed genres and styles of writing. He wrote an old-fashioned, conventional novel—*Las Buenas consciencias* (The good conscience, 1959)—between his early experimental ones. In 1962, he published the novella *Aura*, a masterpiece of fantastic literature.

In 1965, Fuentes traveled to Paris with his wife and daughter; they lived there off and on for several years, and it was then that he came to know Mario Vargas Llosa, Julio Cortázar and other Latin American writers. Like his friends, Fuentes found that distance from his country restored his vision and renewed his creativity. He wrote the greater part of his next two novels there.

Cambio de piel (*Change of Skin*), published in 1967, won the prestigious Spanish Biblioteca Breve prize, but the novel was banned in Spain soon after by the conservative Fascist government for blasphemy and obscenity. It concerns a group of four young people traveling from Mexico City to Veracruz, the site of an ancient coastal city. In presenting the themes of modern Mexican identity and the enduring presence of the Indian past, the novel uses collagelike images and techniques borrowed from film, a medium that has always captivated Fuentes. (In the 1960s, Fuentes collaborated with Juan Rulfo and Gabriel García Márquez on films of their stories and later produced some of his own. In 1967, Fuentes served on the jury of the Venice Film Festival.)

Fuentes returned to Mexico in 1969, the year he published the novella *Compleaños* (*Birthday*), a fantastic story set in London that involves parallel lives, ghosts and reincarnation. He also published an influential essay called "The New Hispanic American Novel," which expressed and defined the ideas of the Latin American "boom" generation. His *Tiempo mexicano* (Mexican time), a collection of political essays, was published in 1971.

Fuentes's marriage to Rita Macedo had ended in divorce in 1969, and in 1972, he met Sylvia Lemus, a reporter for Mexican television. Later that year, they eloped to Paris where they remained for several years. Their son Carlos Rafael was born in 1973 and their daughter Natascha in 1974.

During the early 1970s, Fuentes completed the manuscript of his novel *Terra Nostra*, which appeared in 1975. It is an ambitious, 800-page novel without any real plot, involving the history of the whole of Latin America. It reaches back to the years before the Spanish conquest of America and then into the future. Although considered one of his best works, it is probably the least read. It won several literary awards, including the 1977 Rómulo Gallegos Prize (Venezuela) for the best Latin American novel in five years.

When Fuentes was offered the post of ambassador to France in 1975, he accepted for several reasons: He had never lost his interest in politics and foreign affairs; he agreed with the government policy of Mexican President Luis Echeverría and felt that he might see some of his own political ideas become reality. A third reason was personal: "This was a moment in my life when my father had just died, and I felt it was a kind of homage to accept an embassy he certainly would have accepted. . . ."

But in 1977 Fuentes resigned in protest over the appointment of Díaz Ordaz, the former Mexican president, as ambassador to Spain. He held Díaz Ordaz responsible for the 1968 Tlatelolco massacre in Mexico City in which hundreds of protesting students were brutally killed. Fuentes was exiled from Mexico for several years following his resignation.

In 1978, Fuentes surprised readers all over the world with *La cabeza de la hydra* (*The Hydra Head*), a fast-paced, exciting spy thriller set in Mexico City, modeled on modern detective fiction, but in 1980, he returned to an exploration of Latin American identity with *Una familia lejana* (*Distant Relations*). In this sinister novel, replete with elements of fantasy and magical realism, memory, old age, doubles and

Carlos Fuentes with his family (Jane Reed; Courtesy of Harvard News Office)

eternal life are explored in the story of a Mexican father and son who encounter their doubles in France.

El gringo viejo (*The Old Gringo*, 1985) was the first Mexican novel to become a best-seller in the United States. Fuentes's novel is set against the background of the Mexican Revolution but with American protagonists. Ambrose Bierce, a North American author, journalist and soldier, mysteriously disappeared in 1914. It was rumored that as an old man Bierce vanished in Mexico after joining the rebel army of Pancho Villa during the revolution. In this novel, Fuentes imagines what might have happened to Bierce and in doing so, explores the complex differences between Mexico and the United States. The novel was made into a film in 1988.

Fuentes accepted several teaching positions in the United States during the 1980s and lived in Princeton, New Jersey, for several years. From that base he traveled widely, lecturing on Latin American writers and on his own work. He has also been a visiting professor at Columbia and Harvard universities, among others, and has been awarded several honorary degrees. In 1987, Fuentes's powerful graduation address at Harvard University criticized the U.S. government's policies toward Latin America. Fuentes has always been a very outspoken and public man, for which he has been critized by some intellectuals, but he is a distinguished and eloquent speaker and is always much in demand.

Fuentes returned to the present with his next work, *Cristóbal nonato* (*Christopher Unborn*, 1987), a darkly comic novel set in the very polluted Mexico City of 1992, the 500th anniversary of Columbus's "discovery" of America. In 1989, he published *Constancia y otras novelas para vírgenes* (*Constancia and Other Stories for Virgins*), five stories that were written while Fuentes was teaching in various countries during 1987 and 1988. Considered to be some of his best stories, their settings vary from the American South to Spain, France and Mexico. The themes are diverse, but they echo his ideas about identity and history.

Fuentes has gradually moved away from Mexico as the subject of

"My upbringing taught me that cultures are not isolated, and perish when deprived of contact with what is different and challenging. Reading, writing, teaching, learning, are all activities aimed at introducing civilizations to each other."

his fiction; the history and identity of all of Latin America has become his concern. He frequently returns to the history and culture of Spain, which is such an important part of the Latin American identity. In 1991, he published *La campaña* (*The Campaign*), a novel set in 19th-century Latin America, a time when nations from Argentina to Mexico fought for independence from Spain and forged new identities for themselves. His most recent stories are collected in *El naranjo* (*The Orange Tree*, 1993), which uses the orange as a symbol of Spain's influence on the New World. It is the link between America and Europe, the past and the present, and the stories themselves. In 1995, he published a novel about a Mexican author's love affair with an American film star, *Diana, o, La cazadora solitaria* (*Diana, or The Goddess Who Hunts Alone*).

Carlos Fuentes has always been controversial. Because of his international past and lifestyle, he is often considered a foreigner in his own country. By speaking out on politics, he has irritated the governments of both Mexico and the United States. His fellow writers have accused him of being a false Socialist because of his comfortable lifestyle abroad. While it is true that he no longer supports Communist regimes such as Cuba's, he also criticizes the United States for its interventionist politics. But he is also Mexico's most eloquent spokesman. Fuentes continues to interpret its history, culture and identity to the world.

Given his international past, it is no wonder that Fuentes continues to live a nomadic life. Although he loves Mexico, he finds it difficult to live there for long periods of time. These days, he lives mostly in London with his wife and children, energetically teaching, lecturing and giving interviews, but he can often be found in Paris, Madrid, Mexico City or the United States. Wherever he goes, he is always writing.

Chronology

November 11, 1928	Carlos Fuentes born in Panama City
1929–34	Lives in several Latin American capitals where father is diplomat
1934–40	Lives in Washington, D.C.
1941–43	Lives in Chile and Argentina
1944	Returns to Mexico
1946	Graduates from Colegio México (high school)
1948	Graduates from Colegio Francés Morelos (prep school)
1950	Studies at the Institute for International Studies in Geneva, Switzerland
1951	Enters law school at the National University of Mexico
1954	Publishes his first collection of stories, *Los días enmascarados*
1958	*Where the Air Is Clear*, his first novel
1959	*The Good Conscience* (novel); marries Rita Macedo; travels to Cuba
1962	*The Death of Artemio Cruz* (novel) and *Aura* (novella); daughter Cecilia born
1965–66	Lives in Paris
1967	*A Change of Skin* (novel); awarded the Biblioteca Breve prize (Spain)
1969	Returns to Mexico; divorced from Rita Macedo
1972	Lives in Paris; marries journalist Sylvia Lemus
1973	Son Carlos Rafael born
1974	Daughter Natascha born
1975–77	Mexican ambassador to France

1980	*Distant Relations* (novel) and *Burnt Water* (short stories)
1985	*The Old Gringo* (novel)
1989	*Constancia and Other Stories for Virgins*
1993	*The Orange Tree* (stories)
1995	*Diana, or The Goddess Who Hunts Alone* (novel)

Further Reading

FUENTES'S WORKS

Aura. Translated by Lysander Kemp. Bilingual Spanish and English edition. New York: Farrar, Straus and Giroux, 1986.

Burnt Water: Stories. Translated by Margaret Sayers Peden. New York: Farrar, Straus and Giroux, 1980. Contains the stories from his first collection, *Los días enmascarados*, including "Chac-Mool," and his later collection, *Agua quemada*.

Constancia and Other Stories for Virgins. Translated by Thomas Christensen. New York: Farrar, Straus and Giroux, 1990.

The Death of Artemio Cruz. Translated by Alfred MacAdam. New York: Farrar, Straus and Giroux, 1991.

Myself with Others: Selected Essays. New York: Farrar, Straus and Giroux, 1988. Essays on literature, politics and the author's life.

The Old Gringo. Translated by Margaret Sayers Peden and the author. New York: Farrar, Straus and Giroux, 1985.

Where the Air Is Clear. Translated by Sam Hileman. New York: Farrar, Straus and Giroux, 1988.

BOOKS ABOUT CARLOS FUENTES

Wendy B. Faris. *Carlos Fuentes*. Literature and life series. New York: Ungar, 1983. Good study of the author's life and work.

Daniel de Guzmán. *Carlos Fuentes*. Twayne's World Author Series (151). Boston: Twayne Publishers, Inc., 1972. A study of Fuentes's writing.

Julio Cortázar (Courtesy Columbus Memorial Library, Organization of American States)

Julio Cortázar

REVOLUTION OF WORDS
(1914–1984)

One of the most original Latin American writers of this century was born in Belgium and lived in France for almost half his life. In more than eighty masterful short stories and five powerful novels, he combined fantasy with reality in a playful and often humorous way. His unusual ideas and subjects revolutionized Latin American and world literature.

Julio Cortázar was an unusual person: More than six feet tall, and extremely youthful in appearance even into his sixties, it was rumored that an exotic disease kept him growing and young. He was shy and kept his personal life extremely private. He loved to travel but sought out back streets and alleyways, small museums and little-known sights. He liked abstract art, photography and film, was a great fan of jazz and played amateur trumpet himself. He was humorous, playful and unconventional in both literature and in life.

Cortázar was born in Brussels, Belgium, in 1914. It was the beginning of World War I, and the city was occupied by German troops. His parents, Julio José Cortázar and María Descott, were both Argentine, but his father was engaged in business transactions there at the time. When their son turned four, the family returned to live in Argentina. The boy was already fluent in French.

Cortázar grew up with his mother and aunt in Bánfield, a suburb of the capital, Buenos Aires; his father abandoned them soon after they returned from Europe, and Cortázar never spoke of him except to say that "he had never done anything for the family."

As a child, Cortázar was sickly, and often unhappy. But he loved to read, especially tales of adventure and fantasy. The novels of Jules Verne, such as *Around the World in 80 Days*, were among his favorites. In an interview he recalled:

> like all children who like to read, I soon tried to write. I finished my first novel when I was nine years old . . . and poetry inspired by Poe, of course. When I was twelve, fourteen, I wrote love poems to a girl in my class."

In 1926, Cortázar began public high school in Buenos Aires. He described the Mariano Acosta School as an "abysmally bad school, one of the worst schools imaginable," but he made four or five friends there who went on to become brilliant poets and artists. They formed a close group during Cortázar's student years, although he eventually lost touch with them.

After finishing high school, Cortázar continued his studies at a teachers' training college in Buenos Aires. He received his certification as a public school teacher in 1932 but didn't find a job immediately. In 1935, he enrolled in the University of Buenos Aires to study liberal arts, and passed his first-year exams, but he dropped out when offered his first teaching job in 1937. There was little money at home, and Cortázar wanted to help his mother, who had worked hard to support him during his youth.

Cortázar was 23 when he moved to Bolívar, a small town in the province of Buenos Aires, and began to teach; for the next seven years, he taught high school literature, and kept mostly to himself. Bolívar and Chivilcoy, where he also lived, were dull places and far from the capital, but Cortázar read hungrily and began to write his first poems and stories. In 1938, he published a collection of poems, *Presencia*, under the pseudonym Julio Denis.

In 1944, Cortázar moved to the city of Mendoza, in western Argentina, where he taught French and English literature at the University of Cuyo. He enjoyed lecturing on some of his favorite poets—Mallarmé, Rimbaud and Keats—and was popular with his students, but Cortázar's life, like those of so many Latin American writers at the time, was interrupted by politics.

Most Argentine intellectuals were opposed to the politics of Juan Domingo Perón, who was soon to become president of Argentina. Perón was a nationalist and distrusted foreign culture of any kind. When Cortázar participated in a student demonstration against Perón, he was arrested briefly.

> In 1946, at the time of all the Peronista troubles, since I knew I was going to lose my job because I'd been in the fight against Perón . . . I resigned before I was backed against the wall as so many colleagues were who held onto their jobs, and found work in Buenos Aires.

It was the same year that the writer Jorge Luis Borges lost his job as a librarian in Buenos Aires.

In the capital, Cortázar found a job as manager at the Cámara Argentina del Libro, a publishing association. He continued to live a solitary life, working, writing and going to movies. Although writing was very important to him, he never planned to earn a living at it; at night, he studied for a diploma as a "national public translator," which required knowledge of legal matters as well as languages. After completing the course work in only a few months, he received his diploma in 1947. From 1948 to 1952, he translated various foreign literary works into Spanish for Argentine publishing houses.

Many young Argentine writers admired European literature and culture during the 1930s and 1940s. They were weary of the traditional themes and styles of Argentine literature—romantic accounts of the country's battles for independence and the civil and frontier wars of the 19th century. Young writers were ready for a change, and they looked toward Europe.

Cortázar yearned to go to Europe, where important things were happening in literature; he was also anxious to escape the growing political tension and artistic repression in Argentina. When the French government offered him a scholarship to study literature in 1951, Cortázar jumped at the chance. At the age of 37, he moved to Paris, where he would spend the rest of his life.

During the 1950s and 1960s, Paris was said to be the capital of Latin America: Writers and artists could meet freely there and share political and literary ideas without fear of repression by their own governments. Cortázar became friends with Mario Vargas Llosa, Carlos Fuentes, Gabriel García Márquez and other writers with concerns and ideas like his own. He learned a great deal about Latin America there, and often commented that when he moved to Paris, he became a Latin American; at home, he'd been only an Argentine.

In 1952, Cortázar began work as a translator for the United Nations Educational, Scientific and Cultural Organization (UNESCO). His job involved attendance at world conferences on a wide range of matters including atomic energy, world peace and education; he then translated the proceedings from English and French into Spanish. He continued this career for most of his life, even after he'd become a well-known and respected author. He enjoyed the exposure to world affairs it gave him and found it a source of ideas for his fiction. He also wanted to remain free to write exactly what he chose and not have to rely on the success of his writing.

Paris suited Cortázar: He often said that he preferred being insignificant in a great city to being important in a small town. Just when his friends became convinced that he was settling into permanent bachelorhood, he met Aurora Bernárdez, also an Argentine translator. They were married in 1953 and moved into a tall, narrow townhouse that Cortázar had remodeled to accommodate his height. Later, he bought a country house in the south of France, where they spent about half of each year writing and translating. Their marriage eventually ended in divorce.

Cortázar had been writing short stories all along, but he was reluctant to publish them—believing them not yet good enough. His essays on other writers' work had already appeared in periodicals in Buenos Aires. Borges had admired and published Cortázar's first short story, "*Casa Tornada*" ("House Taken Over"), in a literary journal called *Anales de Buenos Aires* in 1946. On the eve of his departure for Paris in 1951, Cortázar's friends convinced him to publish *Bestiario*, his first short story collection.

The stories in *Bestiario* all have elements of fantasy: A house is taken over by unseen presences; a woman travels to Budapest to exchange lives with her double, who appeared to her in dreams; a man vomits live rabbits in a borrowed apartment; a tiger stalks the troubled residents of a country house.

Cortázar's stories have a strange, dreamlike quality, but they are also strongly rooted in realism. His language is conversational, ordinary and direct; the characters are everyday people—a nurse, a writer, a teenage girl. Cortázar describes their daily lives and routines in precise detail. Just when the reader feels comfortable, something bizarre happens. Most stories have several possible meanings and ambiguous endings that add richness to much of Cortázar's fiction.

The author once said that translating one's favorite authors was the best way to learn how to write. In 1956, he published the first Spanish version of the complete stories of Edgar Allan Poe (1809–49), the American master of the horror story and an important influence on Cortázar's writing. But Cortázar's stories are less gloomy and not really frightening at all—most are on some level amusing, and all of them leave you thinking, just as strange dreams do.

Cortázar believed that the best fantastic stories result from real nightmares, dreams and fears; he described a sense of relief after writing many of his own. In the "Letter to a Young Lady in Paris," a man begins to vomit tiny live rabbits; this relates to a stressful time in Cortázar's life when he was studying for his translating certificate and often felt nauseous. "Bestiary," about a tiger roaming the halls of a large summer house, was written after the author recovered from being ill with a high fever. "House Taken Over" reflects a nightmare Cortázar just had: In it, he fled from noises down a long corridor, locking doors behind him. When he was startled awake by a sound in his room, he hurried to his typewriter without even dressing and finished the story in an hour and a half.

Cortázar's vision of the world was unique. He believed that a second, hidden reality exists beyond our everyday one; this other reality is illogical, mysterious and surprising. The

"Good writing, I think, must tap the subconscious. Writing is imagination, culture, metier, but, above all, it is something you cannot explain. When I write a short story, even I do not know when I begin what the ending will be."

Julio Cortázar (Courtesy Columbus Memorial Library, Organization of American States)

rabbits, tigers and strange noises in his stories are only glimpses of it. They shake up the characters' lives, which have become filled with routine, habit and tradition.

Cortázar was an admirer of Surrealism, a French artistic and literary movement of the 1930s and 1940s that attempted to express the strangeness and truth of dreams through art. Salvador Dalí's painting of watches flying through the air and the unsettling images in the films of Luis Buñuel and Jean Cocteau are very like Cortázar's fiction.

In the 1950s, he continued to publish fantastic stories; some were new, but others had been written much earlier, in Argentina. In *Final del juego* (*End of the Game*, 1956) and *Las armas secretas* (*The Secret Weapons*, 1959), he explored his favorite themes of adolescence, games and otherworldly doubles. The opening lines of "Axolotl" [a Mexican salamander], one of Cortázar's best-known stories, are a good example of how he subtly transforms reality into another dimension:

> There was a time when I thought a great deal about the axolotls. I went to see them in the aquarium at the Jardin des Plantes and stayed for hours watching them, observing their immobility, their faint movements. Now I am an axolotl.

The relationship between art and life is another of Cortázar's favorite themes: In "Blow-up," a photographer's pictures take on a life of their own; "Continuity of Parks" concerns a reader for whom fiction becomes reality; "The Pursuer" is about a jazz musician's anguished attempts to express his feelings in music.

Cortázar continued to write dazzling and expert short stories, some serious, others humorous and always surprising, but "El persignedor" ("The Pursuer," 1956) signaled a change. It is a long story, almost a novella. Characters and ideas begin to become more important than plot and surprise. "The Pursuer" is a brilliant description of a man's search for self-expression: For Cortázar, neither words, music or photography could truly express the human experience.

In 1962, Cortázar published *Historias de cronopios y famas* (*Cronopios and Famas*), a collection of short, very funny sketches. Cronopios and famas are imaginary beings that resemble certain types of people. In brief sketches, Cortázar shows how the cronopios are always late, often sloppy and illogical. The famas tend to be formal, punctual and well-organized. Cortázar often referred to himself as belonging to the cronopio group, by far the happier of the two. The book also includes an instruction manual on such things as how to climb stairs and how to cry.

Cortázar's critics found *Cronopios* superficial at first, but it illustrates much of the author's philosophy of life and fiction. Its sense of play and absurdity are important to his great novel *Rayuela* (*Hopscotch*), which followed soon after and was widely hailed as the first great novel of Spanish America upon its publication in 1963.

Mexican writer Carlos Fuentes called *Hopscotch* "one of the great manifestoes of Latin American modernity." Some critics found it excessively long and overly intellectual, but it was quickly translated into many languages (English in 1966) and became one of the most influential novels of the century. Cortázar had succeeded in breaking many of the rules and conventions of traditional Latin American and European literature. "I was trying to break the habits of readers—not just for the sake of breaking them, but to make the reader free," explained Cortázar.

Hopscotch is an original, complex and experimental novel. Cortázar

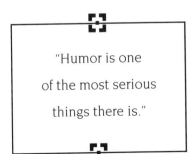

"Humor is one of the most serious things there is."

warns us on the very first page that we are reading something different. Instead of a Table of Contents, there is a Table of Instructions:

> In its own way, this book consists of many books, but two books above all.
> The first can be read in normal fashion and it ends with Chapter 56. . . .
> The second should be read by beginning with Chapter 73 and then following the sequence indicated at the end of each chapter. In case of confusion or forgetfulness, one need only consult the following list: 73-1-2-116-3-84-4-71-5-81-74-6-7-8-93 . . .

The form of the novel is like a game of hopscotch as we skip from chapter to chapter, moving in and out of the plot. The chapters progress in order (1-2-3 etc.) but are interrupted by later chapters (73-116-81) from the end of the book. The later ones (called "Expendable Chapters") are anecdotes, bits of literary theory and news clippings that illustrate or comment on the plot. Because we can choose to read the novel in either of two ways, we participate in its creation. Interestingly, there are electronic novels written for the computer that do the same thing today, more than 30 years later.

In *Hopscotch*, Cortázar experimented with language as well as form: There are pages of invented or purposely misspelled words; the text is full of slang and phrases in French, English and Spanish; he poked fun at worn-out phrases and expressions from Spanish and Latin American literature and also created many rich, unusual and poetic images.

Cortázar rarely wrote about Latin America or Argentina in his fiction. Although he sometimes mentioned the names of streets in Buenos Aires or Paris, place was unimportant.

His characters, as well as his subjects, were no longer local or specifically Latin American. This break from local to international concerns was also revolutionary. After the publication of *Hopscotch*, Latin American writers felt freer to choose new subjects and invent new styles.

Cortázar published three other novels during his lifetime. *Los premios* (*The Winners*, 1960) is a mystery thriller about a group of passengers on a sinister ocean liner that goes nowhere; it is conventional compared to his later novels but has elements of the bizarre. *62: modelo para armar* (*62: A Model Kit*, 1968), an experimental novel based on ideas found in Chapter 62 of *Hopscotch*, follows the lives of a group of strange characters in several European cities and ignores normal time and space. *El libro de Manuel* (*A Manual for Manuel*), about a group of Latin American revolutionaries, was published in 1973.

Like many of his fellow writers, Cortázar believed that socialism was the best solution for Latin America's problems. He had always been a committed revolutionary in the world of words and ideas, but he was often criticized by other socially committed writers for not directly addressing the problems of Latin America in his fiction. In 1970, he participated in a discussion that included the Peruvian novelist Mario Vargas Llosa, another defender of freedom of expression. Cortázar stressed his belief that all truly creative work is revolutionary because it advances the present state of art toward the future: ". . . the most serious error we could commit as revolutionaries would be to want to

". . . One of the most urgent of Latin American problems is that we need more than ever the Che Guevaras of language, revolutionaries of literature rather than literati of revolution."

adjust literature or art to suit immediate needs," he said.

Cortázar became more politically active in his later years. He had visited Cuba on several occasions after Fidel Castro's 1959 Socialist revolution; during the early 1970s, he traveled to Chile to show support for Salvador Allende, the new Socialist president, and he was an active supporter of the Communist Sandinista government in Nicaragua after it overthrew a military dictator in 1979. In Paris, he frequently joined demonstrations at the Argentine embassy to protest the disappearance of thousands of Argentines in the 1970s. He traveled widely, speaking out everywhere against oppression in Latin America. When he won the Prix Medicis for his novel *A Manual for Manuel*, he gave the prize money to human-rights organizations in Latin America. Cortázar's fiction remained relatively free of political content, although he did publish a few stories and essays about the Nicaraguan revolution.

More story collections followed Cortázar's novels: *Someone Walking Around, A Certain Lucas, Octaedro, Unreasonable Hours* and *We Love Glenda So Much*. He also wrote several "miscellanies": Some of them, such as *Around the Day in Eighty Worlds* (a tribute to Jules Verne), are collage books, in which he combined artwork (by himself and others), cutout images, stories, essays and anecdotes.

Cortázar had long sought French citizenship, and in 1981 it was finally granted to him by Socialist president François Mitterrand. He accepted it proudly, but only on the condition that he could remain a citizen of Argentina as well. Despite his long years of residence abroad, he remained deeply loyal to Argentina. Although fluent in French, he always wrote in his rich, very Argentine Spanish.

Cortázar was happy during his later years, which he shared with Carol Dunlop, a young Canadian writer. During the 1970s and early 1980s, they traveled frequently to Latin America together. Like Cortázar, Dunlop admired the cultural progress brought about by the Nicaraguan revolution. She wrote a book about the lives of children there called *Llenos de ninos los arboles* (The trees are full of children), which was published in 1983. In 1981, the two began their last journey together—a playful trip by camper van along the highway between Paris and Marseilles, in the south of France. They brought their typewriters along and recorded their adventure as if they were discovering the highway for the first time. Sadly, Carol Dunlop was dying of leukemia. Cortázar completed *Los autonautas de la cosmopista* (The autonauts of the cosmopike) after her death in 1982.

Cortázar was ill as well, and his health declined in the following years. After a few days in a Paris hospital, he died of leukemia and heart disease on February 12, 1984, at the age of 69. He was buried alongside Carol Dunlop in the Montparnasse cemetery in Paris, amid some of the world's most famous writers. He was the first of the new generation of Latin American writers to die.

Cortázar's fiction succeeds in changing the way we see reality. His writing constantly questions tradition, convention and authority; in many ways, he was a writer of the 1960s when young people all over the world were challenging those very things. His imaginative stories and experimental novels truly revolutionized Latin American and world literature. They continue to be fresh and surprising today.

Chronology

August 26, 1914	Julio Cortázar born in Brussels, Belgium
1918	Returns to Argentina with parents
1926–32	Attends high school and teachers' training college

1935	Begins liberal arts studies at the University of Buenos Aires
1937–44	Leaves university and teaches high school
1944	Professor of literature at University of Cuyo, Mendoza, Argentina
1946	Participates in student protest against Perón and is arrested; resigns from his job
1947	Certified as national public translator
1951	Travels to Paris with a scholarship; publishes *Bestiario*, first short story collection
1952	Begins work at UNESCO as translator
1953	Marries Aurora Bernárdez
1956	Publishes *End of the Game*, short stories; also Spanish translation of Edgar Allan Poe's fiction
1960	*The Winners*, first novel
1961	Visits Cuba for the first time
1962	*Cronopios and Famas*, miscellany
1963	Publication of *Hopscotch*, novel
1973	Publishes *A Manual for Manuel*
1976	Visits Cuba and Nicaragua
1981	Awarded French citizenship
1982	Death of his companion, Carol Dunlop
1983	*Los autonautas del cosmopista*; returns briefly to Argentina for election of new government
1984	Dies in Paris hospital of leukemia and heart disease

Further Reading

CORTÁZAR'S STORIES
All Fires the Fire and Other Stories. Translated by Jill Levine. New York: Pantheon, 1973.
Blow-up and Other Stories. Originally titled *End of the Game and Other Stories*. Translated by Paul Blackburn. New York: Pantheon, 1985.
Unreasonable Hours. Translated by Alberto Manguel. Toronto: Coach House Press, 1995.
We Love Glenda So Much and A Change of Light. Translated by Gregory Rabassa. New York: Vintage, 1984.

CORTÁZAR'S NOVELS
Hopscotch. Translated by Gregory Rabassa. New York: Pantheon, 1987.
A Manual for Manuel. Translated by Gregory Rabassa. New York: Pantheon, 1978.
62: A Model Kit. Translated by Gregory Rabassa. New York: Avon, 1972.
The Winners. Translated by Elaine Kerrigan. New York: Pantheon, 1965.

WORKS ABOUT JULIO CORTÁZAR
Jaime Alazraki and Ivar Ivask, eds. *The Final Island: The Fiction of Julio Cortázar*. Norman: University of Oklahoma Press, 1978. Contains a story and two essays by Cortázar, plus essays on his fiction by leading critics.
Evelyn Picón Garfield. *Julio Cortázar*. New York: Ungar, 1975. The author describes a meeting with Cortázar at his home in southern France and then describes his life and work.
Terry J. Peavler. *Julio Cortázar*. Twayne's World Authors Series (816). Latin American Literature. Boston: Twayne Publishers, 1990. Good overview of author's life and works, with studies of his major fiction.

Rosario Castellanos (Lolo Alvarez Bravo; Courtesy Manuel Alvarez Bravo Martínez)

Rosario Castellanos

THE POWER OF LANGUAGE
(1925–1974)

Rosario Castellanos was born into an important landowning family in Chiapas, the southern-most state of Mexico. Her father proudly managed a vast coffee plantation on the Guatemalan border; dozens of Indians worked for him in the hills and waited on the family in their home. But when Castellanos turned 16, her family lost everything.

Castellanos later declared that it was the best thing that ever happened to her. Obliged to study for a profession, she began university in Mexico City and eventually became one of Mexico's most important writers, as well as a dedicated teacher, journalist and diplomat. She became the most respected woman in all of modern Mexico.

César and Adriana Castellanos were passing through Mexico City when their daughter Rosario was born on May 25, 1925, but they immediately returned to the family home near the town of Comitán de las Flores in the state of Chiapas.

Chiapas is a remote and hilly region, dense with lush forests. It is home to the Tzetzal, Tzotzil, Chamula and other Indian tribes, all descendants of the ancient Maya civilizations that thrived there long before the arrival of the Spaniards in the 1500s. Ruins of their enormous stone pyramids and temples are still being uncovered by archaeologists there, but they are only reminders of glorious lost cultures. Today, as in 1925, many of the Indians live in hardship and poverty.

The Castellanoses were one of the few wealthy families in the region, and they lived like royalty. They made the long journey to the family ranch, Hacienda de El Rosario, under canopies in hand chairs carried by Indian servants. As a child, Rosario Castellanos had little to do and often watched as servant women ground cocoa beans to make her chocolate or spun cotton into yarn for her clothing. She had an Indian nanny and an official playmate, an Indian girl of her own age.

Castellanos had one brother, Benjamín, who was one year younger and her parents' favorite. Because he was a boy, he was treated as the future owner and protector of the family property, wealth and name. He was sent to school to learn about the world and to prepare for his important future. His sister was kept mostly at home.

The landowners in Chiapas followed a rigid, tradition-bound lifestyle. Marriages were often prearranged by the parents. Girls married young and as children were not taught to read or, as Castellanos would later say, to think. A girl's only hope in life was to become a wife and mother, and her worst fear was to end up a spinster, or old maid.

From a young age, Rosario Castellanos felt ignored and unloved. Often lonely, she sought out her nanny for comfort, spending hours watching her work, asking her questions and above all listening to her stories. This Indian woman was probably the most important person in her childhood. Her first novel, *The Nine Guardians*, begins and ends with her "Nana."

Castellanos's mother scolded her when she found her daughter reading in her father's study. She was told to leave the books alone—they were part of her brother Benjamín's inheritance. After that, Castellanos had to steal them and read secretly in the back patios.

Adriana Castellanos believed in spiritualism and had a friend who read her future in cards. In 1933, when the children were seven and eight years old, her friend predicted that one of them would soon die. Castellanos overheard her mother exclaim, "Oh, but not the boy!" Each child began to dream of the other's death, and Castellanos even wished that it would be her brother. When he died shortly after of appendicitis, the family was devastated.

Neither of her parents ever recovered from this tragedy. She remembered them dressed in mournful black, praying and weeping, and was overcome with guilt for having wished for her brother's death. Although often ignored and forgotten by her parents, she was occasionally smothered with attention. She rarely left the house and had no companions other than the servants; not surprisingly, she grew into a painfully shy and awkward teenager.

Castellanos's life in the margins, on the outside of things, turned her into a keen observer. It was during this time that she began to write. At first she kept a faithful diary, in which she recorded details of everyday life in Comitán; these details were useful in her later fiction about Chiapas. Later, she began to write poetry. Her early poems were written for girlfriends at school, who sent them to the boys they liked.

Castellanos wrote in order to survive. Writing became a way of explaining things to herself, of putting her life in order; in her deep loneliness, writing was the only way she

"If I were not a writer, I would like to have been the protagonist of a novel. Actually, that is how I first came to discover my literary calling. I yearned for a kind of existence that was clear, direct, perfect, unalterable and eternal."

could express her feelings. Her first published poem, "To Death," appeared in a Chiapas literary magazine when she was 15.

Solitude and death were often the themes of Castellano's early poems. Her loneliness led her to identify with the Indian servants, who were as ignored and invisible in the family home as she: It was her misfortune to be female; theirs was to be Indian and often female as well. Her later writing would become an exploration of what it meant to be female, Indian—or both—in Mexican society.

In the 1930s, a program of land reform was begun by Mexican President Lázaro Cárdenas that would change the lives of many in Chiapas. The huge coffee plantations and cattle ranches owned by families like the Castellanoses were slowly taken over by the government, divided into smaller farms and given to the Indians who had worked on them all their lives. New laws were passed to help educate and protect the Indians of the region.

By 1941, when Castellanos was 16, her family had lost most of their property. They moved to Mexico City to a small downtown apartment and lifestyle that were worlds away from the space and comfort of Chiapas. The young girl watched as her mother carefully reviewed shopping lists with her father, who questioned each price before giving her the money for market. Her story "Three Knots in the Net" (1971) is a grim description of their life at that time.

But Castellanos finally got her chance to study. Her parents recognized that she would need a profession, now that she had lost her privileged place in society. While living at home, she worked hard at preparatory school and then enrolled in the National University in 1944. Her parents wanted her to plan for a practical, secure profession, and so at first she planned to study law, but she found it too aggressive and political for her tastes. She began to study philosophy instead.

Literature interested Castellanos more than anything else, but she saw little use in memorizing names of writers and styles when she wanted only to write. She hungered for the knowledge and experience she sensed was essential to all good writing. Philosophy did not come naturally to her as literature did, but she hoped to find answers to important questions through its study.

Castellanos continued to write throughout her university years, becoming part of a group of young Mexican and Central American writers later known as the "Generation of 1950." Her poems and stories, which she often shared among friends, began to appear in small literary magazines.

The difficult and painful relationship she had with her parents ended in 1948: Both died within a month of each other—her mother of cancer and her father of heart disease. She had been so sheltered by them that she didn't even know how to light a match, but she was finally free to be herself and to dedicate herself to writing. Castellanos published two long poems that year: "Trajectory of Dust" and "Notes for a Declaration of Faith," both about death and solitude. Although they were praised by some of her fellow writers, she later found them abstract and artificial.

In 1950, she completed her degree and a thesis, "Sobre la cultura femin- ina" (On feminine culture). This was an important work, viewed by many as the beginning of the women's movement in Mexico. It was also the first sign of the feminist concerns of Castellanos's later poetry and essays.

"Literature was so interesting to me that I would look for the important works on my own, and I would figure out for myself how to write. Philosophy, on the other hand, was so foreign to my temperament that only out of obligation would I have contact with it."

In it, she set out to describe women's place in Mexican culture—but found that there was none. Traditional Mexican society was male dominated, with no place for female creativity. Motherhood was the only form of expression available to most Mexican women.

That same year, Castellanos was awarded a grant to study in Spain. During her year at the University of Madrid, she learned a great deal about her native country by comparing Spanish customs and lifestyles to those she knew in Mexico. Like many other writers, she came to understand her culture and herself much better from afar.

Castellanos traveled through Europe with her friend Dolores Castro before returning to Mexico in 1951. Her growing awareness of herself and the world led her to think more and more about the Chiapas she had known as a child, and upon her return she went back to Chiapas to work as "cultural organizer" for the Institute of Sciences and Arts in the town of Tuxtla Gutiérrez. She gave classes in Latin American literature, began a film club and lecture series and expanded the library. But after only a short time she became ill with tuberculosis and was forced to return to Mexico City where she spent nearly a year recovering, first in a hospital and then at home.

She put that year to good use, both as a reader and a writer: Castellanos's first collection of poetry, *Rescate del mundo* (Rescue of the world), was published in 1952. These poems

"I believed that because I had abandoned Chiapas at the age of sixteen and had gone to live in Mexico City far away from those people and their problems, I would be moved to write about very intellectual people and problems. It wasn't so. The people who struggled to appear in my writing were those of Chiapas."

were different than her earlier abstract ones: They were intense, direct and personal. She had found a style of her own. Two more grants were awarded her, in 1953 and 1954, which allowed her to write poetry, do research on women in Mexico and begin her first novel.

In 1956, Castellanos returned to Chiapas to become director of the puppet theater Teatro Petul, sponsored by the National Indigenous Institute in San Cristóbal de las Casas. Its purpose was to teach the Indians about nutrition, health care and legal rights. Castellanos wrote some of the scripts herself. For two years, she traveled on horseback to remote Indian villages, accompanied by young Indian assistants. They carried their own props over dangerous mountain roads to tiny villages and market towns. This experience gave her direct contact with the rich Indian cultures she would later write about. Petul, the puppet character, became well loved everywhere he went. She would later say that these years were the most important of her life.

In her spare moments, Castellanos worked on her first novel. When *Balún Canán* (*The Nine Guardians*) appeared in 1957, it won the Mexican Critics' prize for the best novel of the year. In 1958, it was awarded the Chiapas Prize and was translated into English.

Balún-Canán was the name the Indians gave to the ancient Mayan villages of Chiapas. Taking place during the time of the Cárdenas land reforms, it describes a family much like Castellanos's own. Two of the novel's three parts are told by a girl of seven, very much like the author as a child, who observes the unjust world around her without fully understanding it:

> Lounging in the hammock on the veranda, my father receives the Indians. They approach one by one and offer their foreheads for him to touch with the three middle fingers of his right hand. Then they return to the

respectful distance where they belong. . . . My father dismisses the Indians with a gesture and lies on the hammock, reading. I see him now for the first time. He's the one who gives the orders and owns things. . . ."

The young narrator spends much of her time in the kitchen, corridors and patios with her "Nana" and other Indian servants who relate ancient legends, beliefs and superstitions to her. Nana also tells her secret family stories, like that of the girl cousin who was lured into the mountains by evil spirits and never seen again.

Other Mexican novelists had written about the lives of Indians before, and were labeled "indigenous writers." They tried to portray the Indians as victims of history and injustice, but the characters they created were often false and idealized. Rosario Castellanos did something different: The people she described were well known to her as a child, and so they had all the strengths and weaknesses of real people.

The style of *The Nine Guardians* is simple, direct and realistic. Castellanos's writing is full of her unique powers of observation, and has the magic and poetry of a child's vision:

> . . . And when I stand up straight I can see my father's knees just in front of me. But not higher. He must, I suppose, go on growing like a big tree, and in its topmost branch a very small tiger is hiding. My mother is different. Birds wander through her hair—so black and thick and curly—and they like it there, and they linger.

Castellanos was interested above all in human relationships, which in her experience, were often full of conflict. Social conventions and rules determine how people treat one another in all her stories and novels. In *The Nine Guardians*, a Spanish-speaking Indian is jeered at in public for using the

Rosario Castellanos
(Lolo Alvarez Bravo;
Courtesy Manuel Alvarez
Bravo Martínez)

"white man's" language; yet her mother believes her Indian
servants to be stupid because they can't learn to speak it.

Castellanos followed her successful first novel with two
more works set in Chiapas. *Ciudad real* (*City of Kings*, 1960)
is a collection of ten stories that center on conflicts between
Indians and whites in the region. Her 1962 novel *Oficio de
tinieblas* (of which only parts are translated into English) is
based on an uprising by the Chamula Indian tribe in 1867.

Critics consider these works to be the best examples of indigenous writing to come out of Latin America.

In 1957, Castellanos left Chiapas to return to Mexico City. At 32, an age considered old for women at the time, she finally married. Her husband, Ricardo Guerra, a professor of philosophy at the University of Mexico, respected Castellanos's writing and urged her to continue. But theirs was a difficult marriage, which Castellanos soon viewed as a failure. The couple was divorced in 1971.

In Mexico City, Castellanos continued her work for the National Indigenous Institute, preparing textbooks for Indian children. She wanted children of her own but suffered two painful miscarriages. The poems in *Lívida luz* (Livid light, 1960) are dedicated to the unborn daughter of the second pregnancy and reflect her feelings of grief and solitude. Finally, in 1961, her son Gabriel was born.

The 1960s were busy years for Castellanos. In 1961, she won the Xavier Villarrutia prize for *Lívida luz*. She recalled: "In October 1961, the same night in which I won the Xavier Villarrutia prize, my son Gabriel was born. Among baby bottles and diapers I wrote the prologues to the *Vida* of Saint Teresa, the poetry anthology of Sor Juana, the novel *Les Liaisons dangereuses* by Choderlos de Laclos. . . ." In addition to raising her young son, she worked as press director for the National University of Mexico from 1960 to 1966 and was professor of comparative literature there as well. In 1967, she was a visiting professor in Latin American literature at the universities of Wisconsin, Indiana and Colorado.

Like many other Latin American writers, Castellanos practiced journalism as well as fiction and poetry. In 1963, she began to write essays for the Mexican newspapers *Novedades* and *Siempre!* Her subjects were other writers, art and culture in general. She also wrote about herself, Chiapas, motherhood and women's role in society. Many of these essays were later collected and published in four separate volumes.

In 1964, Castellanos published another collection of stories, *Los convidados de agosto* (The guests of August). Although set in Chiapas like her other stories, their focus is no longer Indian life but the situation of white women in stifling provincial towns. They are often used as objects by the fathers, brothers and husbands who control their lives in their very traditional society.

By the mid-1960s, Castellanos's style had begun to change: The solitude and melancholy that pervaded her earlier work gave way to a lighter tone. Although she was still concerned with the hardships faced by women in a man's world, she began to use humor and irony to expose injustice. In 1971, her volume of essays called *Mujer que sabe latín* (Woman who knows Latin) appeared. The title comes from a popular refrain: "A woman who knows Latin will never catch a husband or come to any good end" and is used with irony. In one of these essays, she affirms: "One must laugh, then, since laughter, as we know, is the first manifestation of freedom."

This ironic approach to women's problems became common in Castellanos's many essays, her two plays and her last stories. One of the most widely read of these stories is "Cooking Lesson," from the collection *Album de familia* (Family album) of 1971. In it, a new wife contemplates her kitchen, trying to decide what to cook for her husband for the first time:

> What do I care? My place is here. I've been here from the beginning of time. . . . I wandered astray through classrooms, streets, offices, cafes, wasting my time on skills that now I must forget in order to acquire others. For example, choosing the menu.

She then goes on to attack and expose the many symbols of women's oppression in modern Mexican society.

The reasons for this change in Castellanos's style appear to be linked to her personal life: Her divorce from her husband in 1971 came as a relief after many years of unhappiness and her loneliness had lessened in the happy companionship of her son Gabriel. That same year she was offered the post of ambassador to Israel and moved to Tel Aviv with her son.

Those who knew Castellanos well said that while she had no political ambitions, she realized that an ambassadorship was an unusual opportunity for a woman in Mexico. She felt obliged to accept, and she proved to be a skilled, efficient and well-loved diplomat. She was also a popular professor of Mexican literature at the Hebrew University in Jerusalem.

The years in Israel were happy ones for Rosario Castellanos and her son Gabriel. The fresh start left her freer to write, teach and work than she had ever been before. She continued to publish essays on women's cultural issues regularly in *Excelsior* and other Mexican newspapers. She completed a comic and experimental play, *El eterno feminino* (*The Eternal Feminine*), which was published after her death.

On August 7, 1974, Rosario Castellanos was electrocuted in her Tel Aviv home while trying to fix a lamp. She was only 49 years old. In Mexico, her death was a cause for national mourning. As a final honor, she was the first woman to be buried in the Tomb of National Heroes.

Her last essays from Tel Aviv appeared in the Mexican press soon after her death. Two collections of essays and her play were published in 1974 and 1975; one novel, with which she was unsatisfied, remains unpublished. Many theses, essays and studies of Castellanos have appeared since then, and a museum dedicated to her life and work has been opened in Tuxtla Gutiérrez, Chiapas.

Chronology

May 25, 1925	Rosario Castellanos born in Mexico City, but family returns immediately to Chiapas, southern Mexico
1926	Brother Benjamín born
1933	Benjamín dies of appendicitis
1941	Family loses their ranch and moves to Mexico City
1944	Begins studies at the National Autonomous University of Mexico
1948	Death of her parents; publishes two long oems "Trajectory of Dust" and "Notes for a Declaration of Faith"
1950	Completes her studies and thesis "Sobre la cultura feminina" ("On feminine culture"); studies in Spain and travels in Europe
1951	Moves to Chiapas to work as a cultural organizer; returns to Mexico City to recover from tuberculosis
1953–55	Receives grants to do research on women in Mexican culture and to begin work on her first novel
1956	Works for the National Indigenous Institute in Chiapas, traveling with an educational puppet theater
1958	Returns to Mexico City; marries Ricardo Guerra; publishes her first novel, *The Nine Guardians*
1960	*City of Kings* (short stories); *Lívida luz* (poems)
1961	Son Gabriel born after two miscarriages
1962	*Oficio de tinieblas* (novel)

1964	*Los convidados de agosto* (stories)
1967	Visiting professor at U.S. universities
1971	Divorced from her husband; accepts post as ambassador to Israel; *Album de familia* (stories); *Mujer que sabe latín* (essays)
1972	*Poesía no eres tu* (Poetry Is not you, collected poems)
August 7, 1974	Dies in Tel Aviv, Israel, from an electrical accident

Further Reading

CASTELLANOS'S WORKS

Another Way to Be: Selected Works of Rosario Castellanos. Edited and translated by Myralyn F. Allgood. Athens & London: The University of Georgia Press, 1990. Includes selections from the novels *The Nine Guardians* and the untranslated *Oficio de tinieblas*; the short stories "Three Knots in the Net," "The Luck of Teodoro Mendez Acubal," "The Cycle of Hunger"and "Cooking Lesson"; many poems and several essays. Good introduction to Castellanos's life and work, with bibliography.

City of Kings. Translated by Robert S. Rudder and Gloria Chacón de Arjona. Series: Discoveries. Pittsburgh: Latin American Literary Review Press, 1992. Contains the 10 stories: "Death of the Tiger," "The Truce," "Aceite guapo," "The Luck of Teodoro Méndez Acubal," "Modesta Gómez," "Coming of the Eagle," "The Fourth Vigil," "The Wheel of Hunger," "The Gift, Refused" and "Arthur Smith Finds Salvation."

The Nine Guardians: a novel. Translated from the Spanish with a preface by Irene Nicholson. Columbia, La.: Readers International, 1992.

A Rosario Castellanos Reader: An Anthology of Her Poetry, Short Fiction, Essays, and Drama. Edited and with a Critical Introduction by Maureen Ahern. Translated by Maureen Ahern and Others. The Texas Pan American Series. Austin: University of Texas Press, 1988. Includes the short stories "The Eagle" (also transl. as "The Coming of the Eagle"), "Three Knots in a Net," "Fleeting Friendships," "The Widower Roman" and "Cooking Lesson"; some of her best poems and essays, and her play "The Eternal Feminine." Very good general introduction; bibliography.

WORKS ABOUT ROSARIO CASTELLANOS
Joanna O'Connell. *Prospero's Daughter: The Prose of Rosario Castellanos*. The Texas Pan American Series. Austin: University of Texas Press, 1995. The most thorough study in English of Castellanos's fiction and essays.

Although there are many books about Rosario Castellanos in Spanish, there are few major studies in English. There are chapters or sections about her in the following works on women writers:

Lucia Fox-Lockert. *Women Novelists in Spain and Spanish America*. Metuchen, N.J.: The Scarecrow Press, Inc., 1979. Contains a description of the social issues present in *The Nine Guardians*.
Myriam Yvonne Jehenson. *Latin-American Women Writers: Class, Race, and Gender*. SUNY Series in Feminist Criticism and Theory. Albany: State University of New York Press, 1995.
Naomi Lindstrom. *Women's Voice in Latin American Literature*. Washington, D.C.: Three Continents Press, 1989.

Mario Vargas Llosa (Michael A. Milkovich)

Mario Vargas Llosa

STORYTELLER OF PERU (1936–)

Mario Vargas Llosa's passion for books began when he was a child. Like many young boys, he loved adventure stories and read as many as he could find, but he hated for them to end, and invented new chapters and endings for them. During his teenage years, he began to write poems, but when his father discovered them he sent Mario away to a military academy to "learn to be a man." He viewed literature as an unacceptable profession for his son.

Luckily, Vargas Llosa was a rebel at heart. He turned the unhappy experience he had at the military academy into his first novel, which was a great success. He went on to write, in an innovative, highly crafted style, many brilliant stories and novels about Peru and Latin America. Today, he is one of Latin America's best known writers.

Jorge Mario Pedro Vargas Llosa (Mario) was born in 1936 in Arequipa, a desert city in the south of Peru. His father had abandoned his mother shortly before his birth, and the boy was told he was dead. When he was one year old, his mother, Dora Llosa, took him to live in Bolivia, where his grandfather worked as an agricultural advisor.

Vargas Llosa was a happy child, doted on by his mother, grandparents and several aunts and uncles. He spent all his time reading exotic action-filled novels by Alexandre Dumas, Victor Hugo, Jules Verne and Emilio Salgari, as well as legends of the Incas, the original Indian inhabitants of the region.

Peru was once the heart of the Inca Empire. The Incas built a rich civilization that grew to include parts of Chile, Argentina, Bolivia and Ecuador before the Spaniards conquered them in the early 1500s. Remains of great Inca stone fortresses and temples survive high in the Andes; rumors of cities of gold and hidden treasure have attracted adventurers, archaeologists and thieves to Peru for hundreds of years.

Under Spanish rule, Peru continued to thrive. Lima was the impressive colonial capital of the New World, the site of the first university and printed book in all the Americas. But today, Peru is one of the poorest countries in all of Latin America.

When Vargas Llosa was nine, he returned to Peru with his mother and grandparents. From 1945 to 1946, they lived in Piura, a small city in the northern desert, where his grandfather had been named mayor. It became a very special place for the author, and is the setting for his novel *La casa verde* (*The Green House*). It was there that he saw the sea for the first time.

One day when Vargas Llosa was 11, his mother told him that his father, Ernesto Vargas, was still alive and that they were going out to see him. The youth was curious and excited, but his father was stern and domineering from the start. His parents reunited shortly after, and in 1946 they relocated to Lima, Peru's capital on the central Pacific coast.

Vargas Llosa hated Lima from the beginning and was very unhappy there: His grandparents, with whom he had always lived, had remained behind in Piura along with his favorite uncle, aunt and cousins. Suddenly, he was forced to obey his father, a severe man who was a stranger to him. His parents' already difficult relationship was made worse by his father's jealousy of the youth's close relationship with his mother. Vargas Llosa grew sullen and rebellious and looked more than ever to books for escape and adventure. He was sent to a Catholic boys' school where he made friends and shared the adventure of growing up. His 1967 novel, *Los cachorros* (*The Cubs*), is based on this time in his life.

In 1950, when Vargas Llosa was 14, his father discovered some poems he had written, and became furious. Against his mother's wishes, the boy was sent to board and study at the Leoncio Prado Military Academy in Lima. Vargas Llosa later remembered that his father ". . . feared for my future (a poet is doomed to die of hunger) and for my 'manhood.'"

Ernesto Vargas meant for his son to learn discipline and strength, but the boy suffered greatly in the rough and aggressive environment. The students were often cruel and brutal to each other, organizing themselves into secret gangs with leaders and slaves, strict rules and extreme punishment. In his memoir, *A Writer's Reality*, he recalls:

> I found the restrictions, the military discipline and the brutal, bullying atmosphere unbearable. But I think that in those two years I learned about the real society of Peru, with its contrasts, tensions, prejudices, abuses and resentments—the one that a boy from Miraflores [his middle-class neighborhood] might never even suspect existed. . . . I immediately felt that kind of experience was what I needed in order to write my own novel of adventure.

Peru is a large and diverse country, made up of immense deserts along the Pacific coast, the cold and rocky Andes Mountains and the tropical forests of the Amazon. Peruvians are Indian, black, Asian and white and speak Quechua, Aymara and other Indian languages, as well as Spanish. But the Spanish-speaking, white middle class has always governed the country and its wealth. The Leoncio Prado Military Academy was one of the few institutions open to all classes of Peruvians. Vargas Llosa's experiences there helped to open his eyes to the complex reality of his country.

Vargas Llosa's writing career actually began at the military school when his classmates paid him to write love letters to their girlfriends. He wrote a play called *La huída del Inca* (The flight of the Inca), which he later produced at another school. Vargas Llosa's first novel, *La cuidad y los perros* (*The Time of the Hero*), is based on his experiences during those painful two years in his life.

Vargas Llosa first began to work as a journalist when he was 15 years old. He had finally convinced his father to let him leave military school, and in the summer of 1951, his father got him a job as a newspaper reporter in Lima. Ernesto Vargas seemed to believe that journalism was a more masculine occupation than writing poetry. The young reporter was in charge of writing police news for *La Crónica*, a job that took him to Lima's seedy underworld of prostitution, crime and corruption and helped him grow up very quickly. His novel *Conversación en la Catedral* (*Conversation in the Cathedral*) depicts the Lima he came to know during that time.

"The books ended, but their intensely vivid worlds full of marvelous presences continued to whirl around in my brain, and I translated myself to them again and again in my imagination and spent hours there. . . . From an early age, I had that ability to take leave of everything around me to live in a world of fantasy, to re-create through imagination the make-believe stories that held me spellbound. . . ."

In 1952, Vargas Llosa returned to Piura, where he lived with an aunt and uncle and continued high school. He led a student strike, which he later wrote about in one of his early short stories, "The Leaders," and directed a successful school production of his play, *La huída del Inca*. After school he worked for a local newspaper, *La Industria*, editing news bulletins and writing editorials. Memories of this time appeared years later in his novel *La casa verde* (*The Green House*).

In 1953, Vargas Llosa returned to Lima and enrolled in San Marcos University, a public school, against the wishes of his parents. They expected him to attend the private Catholic University along with the sons and daughters of other good middle-class families. San Marcos had a reputation for political activism, and its students came from all social classes. Vargas Llosa later explained his choice: "In the romantic way that children discover prejudice and social inequality, I had discovered, in my last year of high school, that the country had severe social problems. I wanted to be identified with the poor and to be part of a revolution that would bring justice to Peru." Because he still didn't believe he could make a career out of writing, he studied law as well as literature.

At that time, Peru was ruled by General Manuel Odría (1948–56), a corrupt military dictator. During those years, Vargas Llosa became active politically, like many other university students. He joined the Communist Party, which promoted an equal sharing of wealth among workers and the abolition of private property. Like other Latin American writers at the time, he came to believe that some form of communism or socialism was the solution to Latin America's serious social problems, but from the beginning, he disagreed with the official Communist Party rule that literature promote only political ideas. His belief in artistic freedom of expression deepened over the years, and he became a firm supporter of democracy.

In 1955, at the age of 19, Vargas Llosa scandalized his family once again by eloping. His wife Julia Urquidi, more than 10 years older than he, was divorced and the sister of an uncle's wife. Vargas Llosa was still in school and had to keep several part-time jobs to support himself and his wife; he worked as a cemetery guardian, librarian, and news and radio scriptwriter at the Panamericana radio station. All the while, he dreamt of becoming a novelist. His novel *La tía Julia y el escribidor* (*Aunt Julia and the Scriptwriter*) is partially about this stressful period in his life.

Vargas Llosa's short stories began to appear in literary magazines and newspapers in 1957. Most of these early stories concern adolescent boys struggling to become adults and describe friendship, violence and social injustice in modern Lima. Vargas Llosa admired the writing of Ernest Hemingway, whose irealistic style and dialogue strongly influenced his own.

He also edited the literary journals *Literatura* and *Cuadernos de composición* with some of his friends. In 1958, he received his degree in literature and won the first of many literary prizes, this one sponsored by the *Revue française* for his story "The Challenge," a vivid, tragic account of a duel between rival gang members in Lima.

The award was a trip to Paris. Vargas Llosa had dreamt of going there ever since he had read the novels of French writers Jules Verne, Alexandre Dumas and Victor Hugo as a child. He spent a wonderful month in Paris, exploring art museums and the bookstalls along the Seine. He even caught a glimpse of Jean Paul Sartre, one of his favorite authors. It was the first and shortest of Vargas Llosa's many journeys away from his native Peru.

Soon after returning to Lima, Vargas Llosa was awarded a scholarship to study literature in Spain. But just before

Mario Vargas Llosa
(Courtesy *World Literature Today*)

leaving for Madrid, he was invited to join an anthropological expedition to the Peruvian Amazon that proposed to study some Indian tribes living in a remote jungle area. That journey was an intense and unforgettable experience for the young writer. It came as a great shock to him that not far from modern, middle-class Peru, tribes of Indians were living in primitive, stone-age conditions. He witnessed how other Peruvians took advantage of the Indians' innocence, stealing their land and enslaving them on rubber plantations. Vargas Llosa's novels *The Green House* and *The Storyteller* are based on this and later trips he made to the Peruvian Amazon.

At this point in his life, Vargas Llosa had lived through most of the experiences that would become the basis of his future fiction. He knew about cruelty and friendship among boys growing up in a chauvinistic society, and had witnessed the discrimination suffered by Indian and mestizo Peruvians who were not part of the white middle class. He had firsthand knowledge of corruption in the government and in the military. He knew the gritty reality of modern day Lima and the beautiful and primitive life of the Amazon jungle. Much of Vargas Llosa's fiction would become a powerful protest against the injustice he saw everywhere in Peru.

From 1958 to 1959, Vargas Llosa and his wife Julia lived in Madrid, Spain. He began work on a thesis about Nicaraguan poet Rubén Darío, which he never finished, but in 1959, he published his first book, *Los jefes* (*The Leaders*), a story collection that won the Spanish Leopoldo Alas award. That same year, they moved to Paris.

Once in Paris, Vargas Llosa applied for another scholarship from Peru, but it was not granted, and the couple spent a difficult and penniless few months there. Finally, he found a job teaching Spanish at a Berlitz language school. At night, he prepared news bulletins about Latin America for a French radio and tele-

"... Patricia and I were embarking for Europe, on the morning of June 13, 1990. When the plane took off and the infallible clouds of Lima blotted the city from sight and we were surrounded only by blue sky, the thought crossed my mind that this departure resembled the one in 1958, which had so clearly marked the end of one stage of my life and the beginning of another, in which literature came to occupy the central place."

vision network where his wife Julia worked during the day as a secretary.

Vargas Llosa had begun what would eventually be 15 years of self-exile from Peru. Although he was never in danger politically, frequent government repression at home did not create ideal conditions for writing or publishing. Most of Vargas Llosa's novels were published in Spain, and several of them were banned in his native Peru.

Through his job at the radio station, Vargas Llosa came to know other Latin American writers and artists who were living in or passing through Paris. Writers Julio Cortázar, Alejo Carpentier and Carlos Fuentes were a few of those who shared his concern with revolutionizing Latin American literature. Along with working and socializing, Vargas Llosa also found the time to write: At this great distance from Peru and his childhood, he completed his first novel.

The Time of the Hero was published in Spain in 1963. It was the first Latin American novel ever to receive the prestigious Spanish Biblioteca Breve award. It also won the Premio de la Crítica Española and second place for the French Prix Formentor. It soon was translated into several languages, and Vargas Llosa became an internationally known novelist. An edition of his short story collection *The Leaders* was finally published in Peru.

Like all of his novels, *The Time of the Hero* is realistic in style and deeply autobiographical, but like the favorite novels of his youth, it is also an adventure story. A suspenseful account of events at a military school in Lima, it describes the boys' struggles to become adults and find their places in Latin American society.

The Time of the Hero was praised for its sophisticated style and technique. Dozens of storylines, each following the life and fantasies of a single boy, are interwoven. Many narrators—students, officers, family members and girl-friends—tell these stories. Flashbacks, like those used in films, are used. The result is a fragmented and chaotic but very readable and suspenseful novel.

Until the 1940s, most literature from Latin America strove to reproduce authentically each country's unique life and customs, but by the middle of the century, Latin American society had changed greatly. Cities had become large and chaotic places where rich and poor, whites and Indians fought to coexist. Vargas Llosa was one of the first writers to set his novels in cities and to use street slang and marginalized characters. He invented a new language and style for describing real, modern day Peru and Latin America.

The Time of the Hero became famous in Peru as well as abroad. The author recalled:

> . . . One thousand copies were ceremoniously burned in the patio of the school and several generals attacked it bitterly. One of them said that the book was the work of a "degenerate mind," and another, who was more imaginative, claimed that I had undoubtedly been paid by Ecuador to undermine the prestige of the Peruvian army.

The 1960s were exciting years in Paris and very productive ones for Vargas Llosa. His articles on politics and literature appeared frequently in European newspapers. In 1965, he traveled to Cuba to serve as a judge for the literary award sponsored by the journal *Casa de las Américas*. He also served on the journal's editorial board.

In 1964, Vargas Llosa and Julia Urquidi were divorced after eight years of marriage, and she returned to her native Bolivia. Their separation was difficult, and Julia published a bitter memoir about it called *Lo que Varguitas no dijo* (*My Life with Mario Vargas Llosa*) in 1983. In 1965, Vargas Llosa made a visit to Peru and married his cousin, Patricia Llosa, who had lived with him and his wife in Paris for a time. They returned to Paris together, and their first son, Alvaro, was born in 1966.

Also in 1966, Vargas Llosa published his novel *The Green House*, inspired by a childhood memory of his from Piura: He and his friends were captivated by the sight of a brightly painted green house in the desert sands outside of the city. He remembers watching men enter there at night and being warned against going near it. Years later, he understood that it was a house of prostitution.

As he set about describing the inhabitants of this mysterious place, an idea for a second novel began to interrupt him. Images and stories from his journey to the Peruvian Amazon rain forest were haunting him and he decided to combine stories and characters from these two very different places. *The Green House* is a rich and complex portrait of the several different Perus that struggle to coexist as one country. Many critics believe this to be Vargas Llosa's best novel.

The success of this work was even greater than that of his first. It won several literary prizes, most notably the 1967 Rómulo Gallegos award (Venezuela). In Vargas Llosa's acceptance speech, entitled "Literature Is Fire," he expressed a belief shared by many of his fellow writers: "[A writer must] . . . assume a social responsibility: at the same time that you develop a personal literary work, you should serve, as an active participant in the solution of economic, political and cultural problems of your society. . . ." Throughout his career, Vargas Llosa has continued to view literature as a form of rebellion against the social injustice caused by ignorance and misunderstanding.

In 1966, Vargas Llosa moved to London with his wife and son. He taught Latin American literature at London University and wrote articles for *Caretas*, a popular Peruvian news magazine. The following year, he traveled widely with his family in Great Britain, Europe and Russia, lecturing and teaching. His second son, Gonzalo, was born. At the University of Washington where he was writer-in-residence, he finished a novella called *The Cubs*, based on his early years in Lima. He also worked on his next lengthy and ambitious novel.

Conversation in the Cathedral was published in 1969. A brilliant political portrait of Peru and a critique of the dictatorship that shadowed Vargas Llosa's university years, it became very popular among intellectuals living in repressive governments throughout Latin America and in Spain. Vargas Llosa continued to use many of the techniques he had experimented with in his earlier novels, but with greater skill and maturity.

After teaching at the University of Puerto Rico in 1969, the author and his family moved once again to Barcelona, Spain. There, he completed a book-length study of a writer he greatly admired: *Gabriel García Márquez: History of a Deicide* was published in 1971. He also wrote a fascinating study about how his own novel, *The Green House*, came into being. It was published as *La historia secreta de una novela* (Secret history of a novel) in 1972.

By 1971, Vargas Llosa's political views had changed substantially: Although still opposed to dictatorship, he no longer believed that socialism was a cure for Latin America's problems. The Communist Cuban government that he had once admired had become increasingly repressive; when the poet Armando Valladares was jailed there, Vargas Llosa signed an open letter criticizing Fidel Castro, the Cuban leader. He also resigned in protest from the *Casa de las Américas* editorial board. He believed that without freedom of expression, social justice could not exist.

Vargas Llosa's readers were surprised when he published *Captain Pantoja and the Special Service* and *Aunt Julia and the Scriptwriter* in the 1970s. Both are humorous, highly entertaining novels that were very popular in the United

States, but underlying the comedy are the same serious social and artistic concerns of his earlier works.

Pantaleón y las visitadoras (*Captain Pantoja and the Special Service*, 1973) is a critique of corruption in Peru's government and military during the 1950s. A series of news reports, military dispatches and sensational personal letters are used to tell the story. Vargas Llosa directed a film version of this novel, but it was banned in Peru when it appeared in 1976.

The author's real-life romance and elopement with his Aunt Julia is the basis of *Aunt Julia and the Scriptwriter* (1976), but it is also the story of another writer, Pedro Camacho, a Bolivian creator of radio soap operas. He is an eccentric little man, completely obsessed with his work:

> He's not a man—he's an industry! . . . He writes all the stage plays put on in Bolivia and acts in all of them. And he also writes all the radio serials, directs them, and plays the male lead in every one of them.

The young writer Mario admires the prolific Camacho as he struggles with his own writing. Chapters of Camacho's outrageous stories about love triangles, incest and revenge alternate with the main story about the characters Mario and Julia, but Camacho's characters take on lives of their own, the plots become entangled and chaos ensues. The novel is a clever exploration of how life is transformed into fiction and fiction into real life.

Vargas Llosa and his family returned to live in Peru in 1974 shortly after his daughter Morgana was born. The writer's long self-exile in Paris, London and Barcelona had lasted 16 years, but instead of severing his cultural contact with Peru, his absence had broadened his perspective on his country and his continent. All of his fiction continued to be deeply rooted in Peru and its culture. Like other Latin

American writers who had lived far from home, he came to understand it more clearly from afar.

Vargas Llosa's own favorite among his novels is *La guerra del fin del mundo* (*The War of the End of the World*), published in 1981. It is the only one which takes place in a country and time different from his own. A historical novel, it is based on a series of violent conflicts between a fanatic religious sect and government troops in 19th-century Brazil. Although the facts are historically accurate, Vargas Llosa invented lives and dialogue for all of his characters, creating an epic adventure novel. The theme of violence brought about by misunderstanding echoes those of his earlier works. "Fanaticism is the root of violence in Latin America," said the author in a *Washington Post* article.

During the 1980s, Vargas Llosa added new dimensions to his literary career. He wrote several short plays, which were produced in Buenos Aires, Caracas and New York City. *La señorita de Tacna* (*Young Lady from Tacna*, 1981) and *Kathie y el hipopótamo* (*Kathie and the Hippopotamus*, 1983) concern the nature of the creative act in both serious and comic ways. Vargas Llosa also produced and hosted a weekly events television program in Peru called "The Tower of Babel."

The author's next two novels were set in Peru. *Historia de Mayta* (*The Real Life of Alejandro Mayta*, 1984) is based on a failed revolution that began in the Andes in the 1950s. Once again, Vargas Llosa created a vivid adventure story out of actual events. But it is also a novel about how reality becomes fiction. *El hablador* (*The Storyteller*, 1987) includes many autobiographical elements from the writer's life, and concerns the moral dilemmas of an anthropologist and a writer who study an endangered Amazon Indian tribe.

In the midst of his intense literary activity, Vargas Llosa continued to speak out frequently on Peruvian and Latin American political issues. In 1989, an influential group of friends who shared his views tried to convince him to become a candidate for the presidency of Peru: His 1993 memoir, *El pez en el agua* (*A Fish in the Water*), describes how his wife Patricia threatened never to speak to him again if he did. She believed that both his writing and his family life would suffer too greatly, but once Vargas Llosa had made up his mind to run for president, she supported him wholeheartedly. After an intense and dangerous year of campaigning (his life was threatened by terrorists on two occasions), he lost the election to Alberto Fujimori in 1990.

After the election, Vargas Llosa began a second European exile in London and in Barcelona. There, he continues to express himself freely on politics and literature by writing, speaking and teaching. Writing has once again become the center of his life.

Chronology

March 28, 1936	Mario Vargas Llosa born in Arequipa, southern Peru
1937	Moves to Cochabamba, Bolivia, with his mother and grandparents
1945	Family moves to Piura, northern Peru
1946	Parents reunite, and family moves to Lima
1950–52	Attends the Leoncio Prado Military Academy in Lima
1953	Enters San Marcos University, Lima
1955	Marries Julia Urquidi
1957	Publishes first short stories in newspapers
1958	Wins French prize for a short story, travels to Paris; begins graduate studies in Spain

1959	*The Leaders* published in Spain; moves to Paris
1964	*The Time of the Hero* published in Spain; divorces Julia Urquidi
1965	Marries Patricia Llosa, his cousin; returns to Paris
1966	Publishes *The Green House*; son Alvaro born; moves to London
1967	Receives Rómulo Gallegos prize in Venezuela; son Gonzalo born
1969	*Conversation in the Cathedral* published
1970	Moves to Barcelona, Spain
1973	*Captain Pantoja and the Special Service*
1974	Daughter Morgana born; returns to Peru
1977	*Aunt Julia and the Scriptwriter* published
1981	Publishes *The War of the End of the World*
1987	*The Storyteller*
1989–90	Campaigns for presidency of Peru, and loses in 1990 election
1990	Moves to Barcelona, Spain
1993	*Death in the Andes*

Further Reading

VARGAS LLOSA'S FICTION

Aunt Julia and the Scriptwriter. Translated by Helen R. Lane. New York: Farrar, Straus and Giroux, 1992.

Conversation in the Cathedral. Translated by Gregory Rabassa. New York: Harper and Row, 1975.

The Cubs and Other Stories. Translated by Ronald Christ and Gregory Kolovakos. New York: Harper and Row, 1979. Includes the stories collected in *The Leaders.*

The Green House. Translated by Gregory Rabassa. New York: Avon Books, 1973.

The Storyteller. Translated by Helen Lane. New York: Farrar, Straus and Giroux, 1989.

The Time of the Hero. Translated by Lysander Kemp. New York: Grove Press, 1966.

The War of the End of the World. Translated by Helen R. Lane. New York: Farrar, Straus and Giroux, 1984.

VARGAS LLOSA'S MEMOIRS AND ESSAYS

A Fish in the Water: a Memoir. Translated by Helen Lane. New York: Farrar, Straus and Giroux, 1994. Memoirs of the writer's early years and an account of his presidential campaign in 1989–90, in alternating chapters.

A Writer's Reality. Boston: Houghton Mifflin, 1991. Very interesting essays by the author on his own life, fiction, and Latin American literature.

BOOKS ABOUT MARIO VARGAS LLOSA

Sara Castro-Klaren. *Understanding Mario Vargas Llosa.* Columbia: University of South Carolina Press, 1990. General overview and detailed analysis of the writer's fiction.

Raymond Leslie Williams. *Mario Vargas Llosa.* New York: Ungar, 1986. Good general introduction to the writer's life and work, followed by an in-depth analysis of his fiction.

Isabel Allende (Archive Photos/Horst Tappe)

Isabel Allende

WEAVER OF MEMORIES (1942–)

When tanks began to rumble through the streets of Santiago, Chile, on the morning of September 11, 1973, many feared just another earthquake. But before the day had ended, President Salvador Allende lay dead in the ruins of the National Palace and the army ruled the destiny of the country and its citizens. During the long years of brutal repression that followed, many Chileans were kidnapped and tortured, some of them never to be seen again. Countless others escaped to live in exile in foreign countries.

Isabel Allende is one of those exiles. Her life as a writer was born of tragedy and loss; yet, her novels and stories are full of spirits, dreams and magic.

Isabel Allende was born on August 2, 1942 in Lima, Peru, where her diplomat father, Tomás Allende, was posted. He was the cousin of Salvador Allende, the future Chilean president. Isabel was only three when her parents were separated, and her father vanished from her life. Her mother, Panchita Llona, never explained why, and Isabel saw him only once again many years later when called to the morgue to identify his dead body. Her mother returned to Santiago with her and her two younger brothers in 1945; there they began a new life in the home of her maternal grandparents.

Allende remembers a marvelous childhood in the old family home where she spent countless happy hours exploring trunks and boxes full of yellowing photographs, old love letters and travel diaries. She read anything she could find, from the adventure stories of Jules Verne and Emilio Salgari to Shakespeare. Exotic souvenirs from an eccentric uncle who had traveled the world were scattered in odd places. He would be the model for the character Uncle Marcos, who invented a flying machine and vanished over the Andes Mountains in Allende's novel *La casa de los espíritus* (*The House of the Spirits*).

Allende's grandparents were very important in her life, as well as in her fiction. Grandmother Isabel was a gentle, mystical soul who dabbled in spiritualism. She held seances to contact friendly spirits, predicted the future from her dreams and could move objects with her mental powers. Once, she claimed that the spirits told her of a Spanish treasure buried under the floorboards of the house; after the family pulled them up and found nothing, the spirits claimed it had been a mistake. This grandmother became the model for Clara in *House*. Allende's grandfather, Augustín Llona, was a stern and domineering man who lived to be nearly 100. He was the model for the patriarch Esteban Trueba in the same novel.

When Allende was 10, her mother remarried, and she began to travel the world with her mother and her new step-father—also a diplomat. "I remember changing places, changing languages, changing friends, until I was 15." They lived in Bolivia and in several countries in Europe and the Middle East. When political and religious fighting intensified in Lebanon, the children were sent home to live with their grandparents.

In Santiago, Allende continued her studies at a private high school but dropped out when she was 16. "I was brought up to be a housewife, but somehow I knew that I needed to work because the house was very boring to me." She took a job as a secretary at the Chilean office of the United Nations' Food and Agriculture Organization. Her work brought her into contact with journalists, and soon she, too, began a career in journalism. She became interested in feminism and the women's liberation movement and wrote articles for a women's magazine called *Paula*. When she was only 17, she interviewed personalities on her own weekly television program. Once, she had lunch with the great Chilean poet Pablo Neruda. He told her she was a terrible journalist but had the imagination of a very good writer.

Allende married Miguel Frías, an engineering student, in 1961. Their daughter Paula was born in 1963, followed by a son, Nicolás, in 1966. In addition to her work as a journalist, Allende wrote stories for the children's magazine *Mampato* and a few plays as well. She has described her life then as busy, happy and very interesting. She imagined a lifetime in Chile, even her burial "under a bush of jazmine" in the cemetery outside of Santiago.

Chile is a narrow strip of a country that stretches down the Pacific coast to the southern tip of South America. It has been described as a "geographical madness," where earthquakes, droughts, tidal waves and floods are commonplace. Pablo Neruda compared it to the thin petal of a flower. The capital, Santiago, perches between the snow-covered Andes and the Pacific Ocean. Its first inhabitants were mostly Europeans, as in other South American capitals. Yet, the mountains, forests, and

"I believe that one writes because one cannot avoid doing so. The need to do it is an overwhelming passion. If I don't write, words accumulate in my chest, grow and multiply like carnivorous flowers, threatening to choke me if they don't find a way out."

deserts to the north and south were home to the Mapuche and other Indian tribes.

Since winning independence from Spain in 1817, Chile had been a peaceful and democratic nation, but the large ranches and farms that fed the country were owned by only a few powerful families. During the 1960s, political tensions began to grow. Landless Indians and mestizos (those of mixed Indian and European parentage) struggled for the opportunity to improve their lives.

In 1970, Salvador Allende Gossens of the Socialist Party was elected president of Chile. For some, it was like a peaceful revolution, but his plans for social change angered many. Even though he made powerful enemies by national-izing the nation's major banks and companies, the violence of the 1973 military takeover took many by surprise. Many believe that Salvador Allende committed suicide during the bombing of the presidential palace; others claim he was assassinated by the military. The truth is still unclear.

Isabel Allende had remained close to her father's family and to her uncle Salvador, who was also her godfather. She had lunch with him a few days before the military coup, when rumors about it were beginning to spread. He told her he would never leave the presidential palace—the people had elected him in a free election, and only the people could take him out.

Most of Allende's relatives fled Chile immediately after the coup. Her mother and stepfather remained in Argentina, where her stepfather had been his country's ambassador. But Allende stayed behind for more than a year with her husband, her children and her grandfather.

At first, Allende simply didn't believe that the repressive new government of General Agosto Pinochet would last. But as time went on, it became clear that anyone who criticized the regime was imprisoned, tortured, or "disappeared." She tried to help these victims by secretly passing lists of their names to international human-rights organizations. Eventually, she realized that the military was in Chile to stay and that she was putting her own family in danger.

Allende lacked the courage to leave her aging grandfather behind. She remembers:

> Every day I would sit there in silence and try to find the words. He would say, "Why do you remain quiet? What do you have to tell me?" The last day I kissed him. He would always say, "Hasta mañana" [until tomorrow], but for the first time in his life he said, "Adios."

He was not surprised when she left for Venezuela to begin a new life in 1975.

"Those first days were terrible. I felt very lonely and desperate waiting for my husband to get out of Chile and thinking about all that I had lost. For a long time, I felt like a Christmas tree that has no roots and will eventually die." Allende's husband and children joined her a few months later, and they began a new life in Caracas, where she found work as a school administrator. But she had lost her grandfather, her home and career, and her beautiful country forever. She thinks of her life as being divided in two by the events of September 1973.

In 1981, when Allende learned that her grandfather was dying, she sat down to write him a letter. "My grandfather thought people died only when you forgot them," she said. "I wanted to prove to him that

"When I left Chile after the military coup, I lost in one instant my family, my past, my home. . . . If there had been no exile, no pain, no rage built up over all those years far from my country, most likely I would not have written this book, but another."

I had forgotten nothing, that his spirit was going to live with us forever." That letter grew into a 500-page novel.

The House of the Spirits is the story of four generations of a family much like Allende's own. It describes events that recall the real and tragic history of Chile. Yet, the family is not quite like hers, and the country remains unnamed.

The novel's central character is Esteban Trueba, who closely resembles Allende's grandfather. He is powerful and determined, a wealthy landowner and conservative politician. He is the head, or patriarch of the family. Yet, it is the women of the novel who are unforgettable: Most of the story is seen through their eyes or told in their words. Mothers and daughters—Nivea, then Clara, Blanca and finally Alba—share powerful bonds and intense relationships. Each forsees her daughter's birth and by tradition chooses a similar name for her (all are variations on "white" or "luminous").

Allende tells her tragic story with fantasy, warmth and sometimes humor. Like Gabriel García Márquez, she uses the technique of magical realism to mix marvelous events with a harsh reality. She exaggerates real stories from her family's past and describes them in loving detail. Clara, like Allende's real grandmother, has psychic abilities:

> The child's mental powers bothered no one and produced no great disorder; they almost always surfaced in matters of minor importance and within the strict confines of their home. It was true there had been times, just as they were about to sit down to dinner and everyone was in the large dining room, seated according to dignity and position, when the saltcellar would suddenly begin to shake and move among the plates and goblets without any visible source of energy or sign of illusionist's trick. Nivea would pull Clara's braids and that would be enough to wake her daughter from her mad distraction and return the saltcellar to immobility.

When Allende completed her manuscript, no Latin American publisher would accept it. In an interview, she explained that there was "great prejudice in Latin America with the work of women." In addition, the length of the novel put publishers off, and Allende was unknown. *The House of the Spirits* was finally published in Spain in 1982 and became a great success there and throughout Latin America. Although it was prohibited in Chile, bold travelers sometimes smuggled it in and copies of it multiplied in secret. The English translation was published in 1985 and it became a huge best-seller in the United States. The novel is now well known all over the world in many languages and was made into a major film in 1994.

Allende quickly became the most widely read woman writer from Latin America. She was "the first woman to join what has heretofore been an exclusive male club of Latin American novelists," said the *New York Times* in 1985. There had been good writing by women from the region before—but nothing with the historical sweep and drama of *House* and the novels that followed. Allende had taken on subjects and themes that were typically male in her traditional society, but her viewpoint was distinctly feminine.

The House of the Spirits brought the political tragedy of Chile to international attention. Allende, however, claims to be uninterested in politics; she insists that the social conflict—as well as the magic—she portrays are a part of everyday life in Latin America. Like other Latin American writers such as Mario Vargas Llosa and Carlos Fuentes, she feels the responsibility to speak for those who are powerless to do so themselves.

Although encouraged by the surprise success of her first novel, Allende didn't quite believe that she could make a living as a full-time writer. She continued at her job as a school administrator and at the same time worked on another novel. *De amor y de sombra (Of Love and Shadows,*

1984) is the story of two young journalists in Chile after the military coup. Together, they uncover a horrendous (and true) crime committed by the military government. It is a more political novel than her first, and the touches of magical realism are fewer, but she continues to describe exotic characters from all classes of Chilean society in rich detail.

In 1987, Allende published *Eva Luna,* an adventure story about the life and loves of a remarkable woman. The novel's plot involves social and political struggle in a Latin American country, but the themes are the art and power of storytelling. With three novels published, Allende finally felt the confidence she needed to leave her job and write full time. A collection of short stories called *Cuentos de Eva Luna (The Stories of Eva Luna)* followed in 1989. These tales are all about strong, independent women who use their power in different ways.

Allende had created new heroines in Latin American fiction: Eva Luna, Clara, Blanca, Alba, Belisa and others all make things happen. They have the power to predict future events, to tell stories, to create and to forgive. They influence political events, and they help others to understand life.

Allende's literary style has often been compared to that of Gabriel García Márquez. While some say she merely echoes his ideas, others feel that she builds upon them. Some have called her writing "magical feminism." Although flattered by the comparison, she is also angry that as a female she must be measured against male writers.

During the long years of exile Allende's first marriage gradually broke down and ended in divorce in 1987. While on a lecture tour in the United States in 1988, she met William Gordon, a California lawyer who admired her writing. She claims it was "love at first sight" and moved to San Francisco and married him that same year. Her son Nicolás and her grandchildren live nearby, and her mother, who visits frequently from Chile, is always the first to read

Isabel Allende (Susan Johannsen)

her daughter's manuscripts. Allende describes her as her best friend as well as favorite critic. In her studio, Allende continues a strict schedule of daily writing. Her calendar is full with dates for lectures, readings and interviews.

Allende finds that her life as an exile and foreigner stimulates her creativity. Her first books were written at a distance from her life in Chile in both time and space. "I can only justify *The House of the Spirits* as an attempt to overcome nostalgia, homesickness, to recover everything I had lost, to bring back the dead, to reunite those that had been scattered all over the world," she explained in a 1993 interview. "Looking back, what I was doing was putting my memory together in a place where I could never lose it again. Writing made it all real."

The long military dictatorship in Chile ended in 1989 when Patricio Aylwin was elected president in free and open elections. Allende is now free to return to her country but has adapted well to her new life in California. In 1991, she published *El plan infinito* (*The Infinite Plan*), her first novel to take place outside of Latin America. Although some personal themes and echoes of her earlier writing remain, the subject is new for Allende. It concerns an American man and his family; the tragedy of Vietnam, racial violence and the 1960s form the social background. The novel reflects the realities of her new life in the United States.

"When I belonged to a place, I was not writing fiction. You need the distance to focus. When you are in the middle of a hurricane, you don't see anything. I had all the elements to write *The House of the Spirits* in 1973, and it took me many years and a great distance, not only in time but in space, to be able to focus on Chile and my family."

Tragedy entered Allende's life once more in late 1991. Her daughter Paula, who was living in Spain with her husband, fell ill with a rare hereditary disease. Allende spent long weeks at her bedside in Madrid, waiting for her to get better, but Paula sank into a coma. Thinking about all the things she wanted her daughter to know about herself and her family, she began to write them down for Paula when she recovered.

But Paula never did. Allende brought her home to California and nursed her until her death in December 1992. Although Allende's memoirs had grown to book length, she never intended to publish them, but her family finally convinced her to, and *Paula* appeared in Spanish and English in 1995. It begins:

> Listen, Paula, I am going to tell you a story, so that when you wake up you will not feel so lost.

Allende's memoir is full of pain, but also joy. The colorful anecdotes from her own past, as well as from the lives of all of her remarkable family, are entertaining to read and are interesting clues to the origin of her fiction.

Allende's female characters are always vivid, strong and memorable. She is an exuberant storyteller and weaves her many tales into a rich tapestry. Despite the pain and terror of the political and personal tragedies in her life, she never loses her good humor and sense of hope. Her novels are full of love for life and for words.

Chronology

August 2, 1942	Isabel Allende born in Lima, Peru
1958	Begins career in journalism
1961	Marries Miguel Frías

1963	Birth of daughter Paula
1966	Birth of son Nicolás
September 11, 1973	Overthrow of her uncle, President Salvador Allende Gossens
1975	Exile in Caracas, Venezuela
1987	Divorces her first husband
1988	Is remarried to William Gordon
1990	End of military dictatorship in Chile; Patricio Aylwin wins presidential elections
1992	Death of her daughter Paula

Further Reading

ISABEL ALLENDE'S WORKS

Eva Luna. Translated from the Spanish by Margaret Sayers Peden. New York: Bantam Books, 1989.

The House of the Spirits. Translated from the Spanish by Magda Bogin. New York: Bantam Books, 1993.

The Infinite Plan. Translated from the Spanish by Margaret Sayers Peden. New York: HarperCollins, 1993.

Of Love and Shadows. Translated from the Spanish by Margaret Sayers Peden. New York: Bantam Books, 1988.

Paula. Translated from the Spanish by Margaret Sayers Peden. New York: HarperCollins, 1995.

The Stories of Eva Luna. Translated from the Spanish by Margaret Sayers Peden. New York: Bantam Books, 1992.

WORK ABOUT ISABEL ALLENDE

Magdalena García Pinto. *Women Writers of Latin America: Intimate Histories*. Translated by Trudy Balch and Magdalena García Pinto. Austin: University of Texas Press, 1991. Introductory section on Allende, and interview about her life and work in English.

Index

This index is designed as an aid to access the narrative text and special features. Page numbers in **boldface** indicate key topics. Page numbers in *italic* indicate illustrations or captions. A "c" following the page number indicates chronology.

A

Academy of Rebels   37, 38
Alfaro Siqueiros, David   53
Allende, Isabel   vii, *118*, **119–130**, *127*
   background and education
     119–120, 129c
   chronology   129–130
   daughter's death   129, 130c
   feminist concerns   121, 126
   further reading   130
   journalism career   121
   marriages   121, 126, 129c,
     130c
Allende Gossens, Salvador   80, 119,
   122, 130c
Amado, Jorge   *32*, **33–49**, *45*
   awards and honors   42, 44, 47c
   background and education
     34–37, 38, 47c
   chronology   47–49
   further reading   49
   journalism career   37, 40–41,
     48c
   marriages   38, 41, 48c, 49c
   political activism   viii, 41–42,
     45
   political persecution   vii, 39,
     40, 46
Astete de Millán, Elsa   12, 14c
Aunt Julia and the Scriptwriter (Vargas Llosa)   116c, 112, 113
Aylwin, Patricio   128, 130c
Aztecs   56
Azuela, Mariano   55

B

Bahia (Brazil)   34, 43
Balún-Canán (Castellanos)   91–92
Barcha, Mercedes   24, 31c
Barranquilla Group   22
Beauvoir, Simone de   42
Beckett, Samuel   11
Bernárdez, Aurora   73, 82c
Bierce, Ambrose   62
"boom" generation   v, 44, 55, 56,
   58, 60
Borges, Jorge Luis   vi, vii, *x*, **1–15**,
   7, 30, 37, 54, 73
   awards and honors   11, 14c
   background and education
     1–4, 14c
   blindness   2, 8, 10, 11, 13
   chronology   14
   further reading   15
   marriages   12–13, 14c
   politics   viii, 10, 71
   themes   13
Buñuel, Luis   76

C

"cacao wars" (Brazil)   34, 35
candomblé (religion)   38, 44
Cansinos-Asséns, Rafael   4
Cárdenas, Lázaro   52, 88
Carlota (empress of Mexico)   56
Carpentier, Alejo   109
Casa de las Américas (journal)   58,
   110, 112